Elevate

Stories and Lessons in Academic Presentations that Guide, Inspire and Lift You Above the Rest

Dr. Aisyah Saad

Elevate: Stories and Lessons in Academic Presentations that Guide, Inspire and Lift You Above the Rest

Copyright©Dr. Aisyah Saad Abdul Rahim, 2019.

All Rights Reserved. No part of this book may be reproduced in any form or by electronic or mechanical means including photocopying, recording, and information storage and retrieval systems—except in the case of brief quotations embodied in critical articles or reviews—without permission in writing from the author.

Email: aisyahsaad@gmail.com
Website: www.draisyah.com

ISBN: 978-1794525221 (Amazon.com)
ISBN: 978-9671687505

First published January 2019
Second impression February 2019
Third impression May 2019

For Mama, Abah and my family.

Table of Contents

Prologue

1 Presentations in Higher Education — 1

1. Academic Unicorn — 2
2. The courage to be different — 4
3. Acetates and OHP — 8
4. "Membawang" on Presentations — 10
5. The Power of Visuals — 15
6. Tongue mission — 16
7. Three Zeros — 19
8. Sans Powerpoint — 25
9. Poetry in Motion — 26
10. Empty Your Cup — 31
11. From a CEO office — 33
12. Creativity, Then and Now — 36
13. Doctor, I'm Not Creative — 38
14. Doctor, what's the best presentation software? — 39
15. The Tale of Two Presenters — 44

2 Teaching — 48

16. Earn Your Space — 49
17. Drawing from the heart — 51

18	Power Pauses	53
19	The Magic Number 3	56
20	Interactive Lecture	58
21	Doctor, can I have your slides?	62
22	Presenting to Win	64
23	Remember My Name	71

3 Grants and Research — 72

24	Harness first impressions	73
25	We eat with our eyes	75
26	RM240,000 in 3 minutes	76
27	50 slides in 10 minutes	80
28	Presentation from Hell	83

4 Notes for Aspiring Researchers and Students — 84

29	Winning sketches	85
30	A note from young researcher	87
31	Imposter syndrome	90
32	When there's no drama...	96
33	How NOT to look boring	102
34	Learn from Jack Ma	106

5 Thoughts on Preparation, Design and Delivery in Academic Presentations — 107

   35 Ideas-storming — 108
   36 Finding Clarity — 112
   37 Invite Creative Energy — 117
   38 Learn to say No — 119
   39 ACE That Presentation! — 121
   40 Doctor, can you do a Powerpoint workshop? — 127

6 Proceed, if you dare... — 133

   41 Apples or Oranges — 134
   42 I am Nothing — 137
   43 Life cycle of lecture slides — 138
   44 Stollen recipe — 139
   45 Everyone has a story worth telling — 143

7 Confessions of an introverted educator — 146

   46 What goes behind the screen? — 147
   47 Accepting My Voice — 150
   48 Showing My Face — 151
   49 What are my tools behind the screen? — 153
   50 Mobile green screen unpacked — 154
   51 My students, my inspiration — 155

8 Epilogue — 157
- 52 Before Elevate — 158
- 53 Trust to Elevate — 159

9 Resources on presentation (that I love) — 160
Photos — 162
Acknowledgements — 164

Prologue

Elevate is a presentation book unlike others. It's not a self-help book nor a how-to book on presentations. Written from the perspective of a former academic and trainer, it is a book about inspiring you to create and deliver beautiful presentations in higher education. It is a book about dealing with fears, nervousness and anxiety, mustering the courage to rise above the challenges faced in academic presentations. It is a book about passion, and having the trust to reveal your authentic self and your message to the world. It is a book about why design enhances your core message allowing it to shine.

I wrote *Elevate* with academics and students in mind. It provides new perspectives in various presentations one would encounter in the academic world–keynotes, teaching, awards, research seminars, grants, workshops and Ph.D. Started as a personal quest, this journey has taught me a great deal about presentations in higher education. Told as presentation stories and lessons, I hope *Elevate* will guide and light your way to rise above the rest in the academic world.

1. Presentations in Higher Education

Academic Unicorn

Academics dwell on the security of words. I remember I took a long time before deciding on losing the text and introduce images, I felt vulnerable. My thoughts were:

- What if I forgot what to say in front of my students?
- What do they think of me? A fake?
- What if they don't like my lecture?
- My slides have nothing much to copy from, am I the only one? What if they complain to the Dean that I don't teach? (Fearing for my job confirmation)

But I felt compelled to shake things up. My motivation came from my students whom I saw falling asleep while I give a text-laden lecture, non-stop for 50 minutes. I was a new lecturer, raring to share my knowledge with my students. I thought I had given my best at every lecture.

Turned out, my chemistry lecture was the best drug for insomnia. Tuning out, feigning interests and sleeping were the responses I saw, after several lectures. Those in rows 1 and 2 seemed alert throughout my lectures. Starting from row 3 onwards, students yawned, nodding off and, the last two rows, fallen asleep.

In 'pantry-discussions', I asked my senior colleagues how to overcome this problem of students not paying

attention, in the class. Some suggestions:
- "Let them be."
- "Tell them to leave your class. Say, I won't tolerate this behaviour."
- "Ask them to stand up and do quick warm-up exercises."
- "Oh... that's normal in mine. In my morning classes, I have some students who came to class and read a newspaper or doing something else on their laptops." What did you do?... "I ignored them and continued teaching."

The suggestions, though well-intended, I felt hardly solve the heart of the problem. The problem still bugged me, how do I engage my students and make chemistry interesting? This question is the start of my decade-old quest towards effective and impactful presentations. Ways to engage my students in class became my obsessions.

I then stumbled upon Presentation Zen blog by Garr Reynolds. I studied it, blog entry per blog entry. Torrents of ideas ran through my mind. Garr's way of slide designs—stripping away non-essential text and leaving only what is essential on a slide—a minimalist approach seemed appealing. Can this be the answer to my prayer?

"You cannot discover new oceans unless you have the courage to lose sight of the shore."–André Gide

The courage to be different

"You know I have been following the tips and techniques on Presentation Zen blog. Clean and simple slides for my teaching. I even bought his Presentation Zen book. Then, I saw your teaching slides in the book. How do you get your work featured in that book? Do you know the author, Garr Reynolds?" asked a Dean at one of the top universities in Malaysia.

He invited me to give a mini-workshop on presentation. This question popped up during the break.

A fair question.

"I didn't know Garr personally, but like you, I followed his blog. Then, he announced that he was writing a book on presentation. He wanted to get some sample slides from his blog readers. So I wrote to him," I replied.

. . .

My first email to Garr is as follows:

Hello Mr. Reynolds,

I'd like to share with you my experiences as a lecturer teaching Organic and Medicinal Chemistry at Universiti Sains Malaysia, Penang.

I find your 'Presentation Zen' blog extremely useful in

designing my chemistry lecture slides. I'm quite visual myself, and I wasn't too happy with the bullet-point form of presentation nor was I happy with the OHP.

When I came upon your 'Presentation Zen' blog, I went through each method and tried to apply them into my presentation. The methods that I found most useful are Kawasaki's and Takahashi's. Then, by combining visuals (e.g. pics from stock.xchg.com, chemical structures etc.) with these two methods—I found that the students respond differently to my lectures i.e. they're more attentive. Now, they have to listen more and try to understand my lectures than simply copy things off lecture slides. Wonderful!

I found new connections and thinking I believe wouldn't have emerged if I kept using bullet-points as these would be like using crutches all the time.

Recently, I use a Wacom Tablet as a regular feature in my lecture. This way I can scribble off notes or highlight features on the slides to the students - yeah, it's a great way of interacting with students.

Designing my lectures the way you 'evangelize' helps me a lot—personally and professionally. In my experience, before I could start designing one slide I have to clarify my thoughts on a lot of things - chemical concepts, the story I'd like to tell in that lecture, how to layout the elements of the concepts in the *most beautiful and effective way possible.*

I also found that while doing these thinking, I have to extract enormously from my experience and others before translating them into chemistry. I found new connections and thinking I believe would not have emerged if I kept using bullet-points as these would be like using crutches all the time.and thinking that I believe would not have emerged if I kept using bullet-points as these would be like using crutches all the time.

The challenges of designing slide using the PZ approach are first, the presenter has to have the courage to be different; second, it's time-consuming (each lecture is a mini-evolution of one's thoughts and experiences, rather than copy & paste things) and third, the instructors or lecturers have to thoroughly understand the contents before delivering them. But, so far it's been fun, and I thoroughly enjoy the whole experience and the learning process:-) Lastly, please find a short medicinal chemistry lecture in a pdf format that I designed with the PZ approach in mind.

Thanks very much for all the efforts you put into your blog. They've changed my world.

And I definitely look forward to your first book!

Best regards,
Aisyah

• • •

We had a few more communications on including my teaching slides in his first book. I checked his blog occasionally, but after sometime entirely forgotten about it due to commitments in teaching and research.

Voila! The next thing I knew, his first book arrived in the mail. Aptly titled, Presentation Zen is a beautiful book. A book that is worth savouring slowly. Garr featured my teaching slides as sample slides in Chapter 7. A mix of small and big slides, on a two-page spread; a lovely layout.

One of the happiest days of my life.

Lessons in academic presentations

- If students find a topic challenging, explore why and use it as a starting point of your journey.
- When your spirit arises towards something greater than yourself... Dare to be different. In the words of Rumi, the 13th century Persian poet:

"Your heart knows the way. Run in that direction."

Acetates and OHP

My journey into presentations started over 20 years ago. It started with MS Powerpoint 95. I remember it was during my pre-registration training as a house-pharmacist at Hospital Ipoh. My first encounter with Powerpoint. I was asked to stand in for a senior pharmacist and deliver a short talk to discharged patients on hypertensive drugs. There were acetates (transparencies) available, but I dabbled with this version of Powerpoint. The teaching tips from my late dad helped me design my first Powerpoint presentation.

I remember bits and pieces of my late dad's acetates. One of his teaching aids he would bring home after work. Stacks of colourful acetates and their markers. The markers gave a unique high-note smell. I remember playing with them. Plenty of doodling opportunities. And learning too.

Seeing me doodling with the acetates, my late dad would pull me aside and share about his work. He would patiently explain and show me how each of the coloured cut-outs or layers on the acetates worked to the overall design and contents. How the rectangular cut-out bits would help his students understand better.

Even though I was probably around 10 years old, it made perfect sense. I realised I have been using the same principles my late dad taught me ages ago. The overhead projector (OHP) and acetates may have been replaced by LCD projector and presentation software; the layering approach, however, stands the test of time.

Certain things remain the same; only times have changed.

Over time, I realised there is one presentation tool that keeps letting me express my ideas in a multitude of ways as a presenter, a presentation designer, a scientist and an educator. Beautifully too. It's Apple Keynote.

And my journey continues. In the pursuit for the best presentation approaches and software in higher education.

Lessons in academic presentations

- Layering is a powerful way to direct your audience's focus.
- Design your lecture by breaking down complex information into small units and presenting them one-by-one, as layers in a sequence.
- Where complexity gives way to clarity, you will make learning easier and more accessible. At the heart of a presentation is making things simple, if not simpler.

"Membawang" on Presentations

Today I really enjoyed a 'membawang & lunch' session on presentations. 'Membawang' is a recent Malaysian slang means gossiping. In a village community, one of the pre-wedding activities is peeling off onions (bawang). Performed by makcik-makcik (aunties), they would chit-chat and gossip during this session.

'Membawang' with my friend, Dr. SL, was a welcomed activity because we didn't have to be so academic about it. Yet we learned something about presentations from the session.

We went to a new Syrian restaurant for the 'membawang' session. Initially, we wanted to go to the tasty Nasi Padang International, but it's closed on Friday.

The restaurant turned out to be nicer than we thought. Housed in a refurbished old colonial house, Halab serves delicious Syrian cuisine with attentive wait staff. A great ambiance for catching up with SL.

We chatted about the presentations at the USM T&L Symposium (UTLS). Similar to TEDx, presenters stand on a red circular carpet while delivering a talk for 18 minutes on a current topic. From the 'membawang & lunch' session, we sort of came up with several lessons on presentations. The main takeaways are as follows:

1. Storytelling is the secret sauce for an amazing presentation

SL was telling me about how amazing was Dr Khayriyyah's talk. Dr. Khayriyyah is 2018 winner for the FameLab International Award. The title of her talk was "How To Be HEBAT?" HEBAT is an acronym for Holistic, Entrepreneurial, Balanced, Articulate and Thinking– students' attributes of the university.

Interestingly, she didn't spell out what HEBAT is until towards the end. Instead she told stories that conveyed the message. They are her stories.

Baltimore, snowmageddon, building igloo, writing a letter to an insurance company and her dad.

Seemingly random at first, but turned out to be a careful selection of her stories that made the audience think, laugh and cry. She made the topic so relatable. They elicited people's emotions. That is what a great presentation is about.

She wrapped up her talk by re-iterating her points about creating a goal for yourself. That requires effort. And one can have different HEBAT moments at the university. It's up to oneself to define that HEBAT moment.

2. Keep your visual simple

Still on Dr Khayriyyah's talk. I saw that she kept her visuals simple and coherent with her scripts. I learned that she was at the January 2018 P&P workshop (Pengajaran dan Pembelajaran, *Teaching and Learning workshop*) where I conducted a short workshop on Designing Effective Presentation, similar to a recent August workshop. Perhaps she took some notes.

For your next presentation, find those visuals that help you tell your story more effectively. I love Pixabay and Unsplash. These two sites provide beautiful photos for free and mostly licensed under public domain, CC0.

3. "Can you listen me?"

During our 'membawang' session, we agreed on certain things. If you speak in 'blocks' i.e. incomplete sentences that your audience can understand, they can still forgive you. Likewise, for technical glitches.

However, the lack of practice would look so obvious on stage. High-pitched voice, mumbling and space-fillers can be quite annoying. Add on the microphone effect, which amplifies these unnecessarily 10 times louder.

Another is language fluency. Can you listen me? Umm... that can be a big turn-off for many in the audience. Particularly for such a high-profile event like this symposium. And particularly when the audience are mainly academics.

4. Err... urm... uhh...

I remember the experience preparing for my presentation at a plenary session. A week before the session, I wrote down my script. Then, I read it out loud. I revised the script several times. I practised reading it out loud first with Evernote's voice memo on my iPad mini. I listened to the first recording. I sounded so stiff...

I tried to loosen up with vocal warm-up exercises. I used the exercises shown in a TEDx talk by Julian Treasure. It's a routine of mine before any workshops. Five minutes into the vocal warm-up, I could hear a big difference in my voice. Deeper and clearer tones emerged. I spoke from my centre and not my throat. At the end, I realised I've made like 10 recordings. On the 10th, my speech sounded fluent. Hardly any mumblings or space-fillers. No err... urm... uhh...

I felt confident giving a speech that day at the international conference organised by the university library. With the confidence, I improvised my session by including participations from the 500-odd audience. They were a little taken aback by my questions, but took part anyway. Their responses interestingly concurred with my next slides. Good flow. Can't forget the awesome feeling until today.

Back to the UTLS, my votes for great speech/presentations go to our beloved VC (as always), Professor Dr. Mushtak Al-Atabi dan Dr. Khayriyyah. They spoke from the heart. And that moved people at the core.

Lessons in academic presentations

- To deliver an academic presentation that engages your audience, you need to have a focal point in your message. Using visuals is a simple way to keep your audience focused.
- Alternatively, rather than dumping data or information, exercise restrain by keep to one idea per slide.
- Use carefully selected ideas or focal points as navigational points for your audience, taking them step-by-step to the final destination, without them realising it.

Now that's what I called Harry Potter moments.

The Power of Visuals

"A picture is worth a thousand words" a cliché that rings true in the age of social media. Instagram, Facebook and Twitter, for example, capitalise on the power of visuals. A social media post with an interesting picture or a video is likely to get 10 times more clicks[1] than those without. We eat with our eyes—visuals grab our attention first.

Likewise, a presentation is a visual communication. The power of visuals cannot be underestimated, but in the 'words-centric' world of higher education, visuals seem under appreciated. Such practice is seen on many academic presentations, consequently lead to 'Death-by-Powerpoint' phenomenon—dry and dull presentations.

Lessons in academic presentations

Think presentations as a platform for you to publicise your work and do networking with fellow academics. To gain greater engagement in presentations, learn from social media: present key points with relevant visuals. Keeping them short and sweet will go a long way.

---

[1] The power of pictures. How we can use images to promote and communicate science, http://bit.ly/visual-power, accessed 15 Jan 2019.

Tongue mission

I'm not a morning person. My brain achieves the optimum state of working around 4.30 pm until 6.30 pm and 11.30 pm until 3 am. Not unlike a vampire. Over time, I learned that the ideal time for my brain to start working is 10 am.

At the cusp of the 4th industrial revolution, the time we start working is far from ideal (and it's not a complaint). To adjust, I had to figure out some ways to literally wake myself up for a full day workshop.

My favourite hack is to brew a quattro espresso, then make it up into a flat white. Quattro is four; yes, a four-shot espresso. My stomach would throw a spiteful tantrum if I take my coffee black. Henceforth, I start my morning workshop with coffee. My enamel mug follows me wherever I go.

Over time, coffee doesn't seem to give me enough wake-me up call. Where a sip or two used to jolt me to the morning and everything seems like sunshine, nowadays it seldom does so… A sip is akin to a whisper to me, 'Aisyah… get up…' ever so soft it calls my name. A mug of flat white later, my brain is as clear as a cloudy day.

A scientific explanation to this loss of effects is perhaps oversaturation of caffeine receptors. Oversaturation leads to receptors firing off responses at first (remember? the jolt). But if the overstimulation continues, the receptors get tired (overstimulated) and less firing occurs. Subsequently, no amount of caffeine could help keeping my eyes open and brain to start working in the morning.

Sleeping earlier helps but then I would wake up at 3-4 am. If I go back to sleep, I'm afraid to wake up late and miss the early morning class or workshop altogether.

It's tough when one's circadian rhythm differs from an organisation's. One feels like a zombie walking and talking to a roomful of participants. I'm sure they can see the zombie in the room. Emotionless. Just following the motion in the first session in the morning. If only the participants knew how much I look forward to the morning break at 10.30 am!

One day I chanced upon a TED talk by Julian Treasure. "How to speak so that people want to listen" is the title of the 10-minute video. Another good resource is a course on Udemy "Confidence On Camera: Make Amazing Videos, Easily". Included is a voice lesson. The techniques and tips I picked up from these videos have transformed my pre-workshop morning routines.

More importantly, doing the vocal warm-up exercises help preserve one of the most valuable assets in a presenter's arsenal, your voice.

I learned how to do a vocal warm-up, not only for the throat but also for the voice arising from the chest and stomach. I learned to do facial massages using fingers and my tongue. Extremely helpful to loosen up the tight facial muscles, which allows a smoother articulation during a presentation.

Somehow it feels playful when using my tongue to massage my cheeks from the inside. I would break into a broad grin every time I did this exercise. It puts a positive spin in my energy to start the day. I feel energise and start my workshops in high energy.

These tongue and throat exercises only take 5-10 minutes before a morning presentation session, but the effects last the entire day. Mission accomplished, sans coffee!

Lessons in academic presentations

- Educators receive no training in vocal lessons but it is not difficult to start. A quick search on youtube would lead you to some tips and quick lessons by professional vocal coaches.
- A proper vocal warm-up is highly recommended to ensure smooth articulation. It helps you start in a good mood and high energy that captivates your audience. More importantly, doing the vocal warm-up exercises help preserve one of the most valuable assets in a presenter's arsenal, your voice.

Three Zeros

I attended a captivating talk by Professor Muhammad Yunus, Nobel Peace Laureate titled "A World of Three Zeros" at Dewan Budaya, Universiti Sains Malaysia on 11 August 2018.

It's about his gallant effort in eradicating poverty, unemployment and carbon emission in the world. Oh, I simply love the way he thinks. Brilliant at shifting the mindset of the mass or 'standards' set by the public. Shifting one 'thought brick' at a time. His ideas are simple yet effective. He's good at telling jokes too—especially poking fun at bankers and current practices.

Prof. Yunus started off by saying he wanted to be useful to the world, outside the university. He went to villages to find out what he could offer. After seeing the realities of the outside world, he felt all the courses, classes in economics were useless. For example, there was no mention of loan sharks in economic courses, yet the rural poor were using the 'services' of loan sharks.

To the eyes of bankers, the poor are 'credit-unworthy'. Prof. Yunus argued that the bankers are 'people-unworthy'. Thus, due to the prevailing 'people-unworthy' banking practices, the poor had to resort to the loan sharks for a small amount of loan to start a business.

A brilliant spark

Prof. Yunus, then, had a brilliant spark. What if he starts offering a small loan? In the beginning people asked him whether he is another loan shark? (Hilarious!) Eventually he managed to convince some rural people, and that snowballed into several hundreds and thousands.

A social business is a business with profits for others; as opposed to a business, which aims to bring profits for self. A social business is selfless.

For rural people, a small loan of USD30 means a lot. For instance, a small loan is enough to buy a few chickens for eggs. The eggs can be sold and after certain months, the small loan can be paid with interest. The whole micro-finance cycle starts again. And he set the target to offer 50% of these small loans or micro-credits to women.

But why women? some bankers asked... To this, Prof. Yunus retorted, why men? In many traditional banking practices, loans are provided to practically men. Astonishingly, only 1% were lent to women (in Bangladesh, I think). He set to change the practices for Grameen Bank.

To meet the 50% women lenders, interestingly, Prof. Yunus had to overcome some challenges. He had to convince women to take the money (the micro-credits).

The second Zero is directed for the children of his earlier borrowers— they were university graduates who complained of the lack of job opportunities.

According to him, money is handled or own by husbands. Wives hardly felt they were good enough to deal with money. They would rather remain 'invisible' than to take the risk of managing money. Overcoming these deeply ingrained perceptions took him 6 years before reaching the target of 50%.

Later the 50% target was abolished; the percentage of micro-loans taken by women soared to 97%.

Towards three zeros

Prof. Yunus also explained the concept of a social business. A social business is a business created and sustained to solve a social problem. It is run to cover the cost. A social business is a business with profits for others; as opposed to a business, which aims to bring profits for self. A social business is selfless. He added the 'profits for self' is the underlying assumption of capitalism.

To this end, Prof. Yunus established Grameen Bank, the bank for the poor, a noble effort to help reverse the unhealthy socioeconomic imbalances and poverty in the society by providing micro-loans for small businesses. That's the first Zero. The second Zero is directed for the children of his earlier borrowers—they were university graduates who complained of the lack of job opportunities. Interestingly, Prof. Yunus was accused for 'creating unemployment problems/conditions'.

Brilliantly, he reversed the mindset by saying we are entrepreneurs at birth; never a job-seeker. So he challenged the university graduates to learn to create small businesses—just like their mothers did 2-3 decades earlier. For the final Zero, Prof. Yunus shared his effort venturing into energy, solar energy specifically, for rural communities by Grameen Shakti.

Prof. Yunus acknowledged USM and Malaysia where Amanah Ikhtiar Malaysia started. And where it opened the door for his micro-finance system to get replicated and scaled up around the world.

...he enthralled the entire 400-strong crowd with his stories and intelligent humour.

Before he ended his talk, he puts out recommendations on laying some kind of boundary for technological advances–between a blessing and a curse. Citing the news of artificially intelligent-written short fiction that nearly won a literary award, he believed that unwarranted technological advances can do more harm than good to human civilisation. With that message, he concluded his inspiring talk on 'A World with Three Zeros: poverty, unemployment and carbon emission'.

• • •

Lessons in academic presentations

A brief analysis of Prof. Yunus' presentation: Overall a huge enterprise for the others, explained in simple laypeople's language by Prof. Muhammad Yunus. Before I came to his talk, I thought it is going to be dry. I was wrong as mentioned earlier–Prof. Yunus seemed to enjoy poking fun at bankers (and burst their bubbles).

It's a talk by an economist successful in offering 'his kind of social business model'[2] to solve socio-economic issues involving the banking/micro-finance systems that

---

[2] 'His kind of social business model': he related a story that people say the micro-finance system for the poor seemed successful in Bangladesh, Malaysia and other countries, but didn't seem to work in the States. People said perhaps it's American people, different from the rural poor. He said people needs are the same; perhaps the systems have been tweaked differently. So he sent his branch manager from Grameen Bank to replicate and build the exact same micro-finance system in Queens, New York. It worked.

anyone can relate to and understand. He started with a personal statement i.e. he wanted to be useful to the villagers.

And the fourth zero...

This is exactly what a presenter with strong academic backgrounds should aspire for. Humble, gentle and affable, Prof. Yunus talked for almost 70 minutes with zero slides– his fourth Zero ;-). He used simple English. He spoke calmly with clarity. No macro- or micro-economics jargons was used. And he enthralled the entire 400-strong crowd with his stories and intelligent humour. Prof. Yunus' talk reminds me of Sir Ken Robinson's TED Talk: 'Can schools kill creativity?'

If there is one message of Prof. Yunus that resonates so strongly with me... It's when he said, "The village became my university."

"While technology is important, it's what we do with it that truly matters."
–Prof. Muhammad Yunus

Sans Powerpoint

Today I had an opportunity sitting in as an observer at an Orang Asli (Aborigines) leadership workshop, conducted by Universiti Malaysia Sarawak researchers. The Orang Asli participants were the village heads (Tok Batin) and telecentres staff who came from several settlements e.g. Pos Sinderut (it's called 'pos' in Bahasa Melayu, BM). Immediately, I noticed one distinguishing factor. That participants and even trainers, came in T-shirts, track pants, jeans, flip-flops and sport shoes. No tie, no coats, no corporate attire. They came as they were.

The seating arrangement is different too–they were set in a circular format. An arrangement that encourages community and collaborative spirit rather than individuality. Besides that is the use of translator for the lead facilitator, a foreigner who spoke in English. His message was translated in BM so that it is understood by Orang Asli. That sets the tone for the rest of the sessions; community champions, trainers and researchers delivered presentations and hold discussions, played games and danced together. An impactful workshop without a Powerpoint. A lesson in knowing your audience.

So refreshing for a change.

Poetry in Motion

For years, I had always wanted to swim freestyle gracefully but couldn't go past 2 strokes because floating and breathing seemed impossible. And then, there's so much kicking involved... When I was an undergraduate, I took a few swimming lessons at the Cardiff public swimming pool. Alas... it seemed too difficult; it put me off.

When I went for my leisure swim (or rather a dip?) at the university's swimming pool, I observed a few things. The first few lessons in swimming always start with instilling water confidence. Newbies start with those colourful kick boards, practising floating, vigorous kicks and strokes. A few session later, when they are more confident in water, they swim (using kick boards) across the whole pool yet with vigorous kicking. Kicking in water tires me a lot. Swimming hardly felt enjoyable.

If you watch athlete swimmers, on the other hand, they swim effortlessly and gracefully...

Graceful swimming

And then there are swimmers just slam and splash everyone else nearby as they move. Too much bubbles, too much energy expedited and lost. If you watch athlete swimmers, on the other hand, they swim effortlessly and gracefully through the waters, laps after laps. Watch Ian Thorpe. Little bubbles, sustaining high efficiency strokes after strokes. Swimming like a dolphin and a Labrador in water—the big difference could be due to the methods and techniques employed.

So when I chanced upon Terry Laughlin's online Total Immersion[3] videos, my initial thought was it is a fluke. Nevertheless, Shinji Takeuchi's graceful swimming video caught my attention. Due to amazing reviews, I thought I would give the swimming techniques a go. What have I got to lose?...

---

[3] Thank you Terry Laughlin for sharing the passion, insights and joy in swimming. RIP.

The first lessons in water confidence are simply doing a dead man pose in water. When you get more comfortable, you start to add turning side-by-side while floating. Extending the arm to mimic a swimmer's stance comes next. No kick boards involved, fewer kicks to propel oneself in water. In less than 1 month, I could swim a full 50-metre lap.

A quick glance, swimming and presentation are both skill- and performance-based pursuit; both require years of training to perfect the art.

I kept practising my strokes with the help of a front snorkel while still learning how to breathe side-to-side. This was the most difficult part of freestyle swimming for me—coordinating the strokes, turning my body for a quick gulp of air. It took me another month to synchronise breathing with my strokes. Meanwhile, I swallowed tons of chlorine water... Well, that's a part of the learning process.

Once mastered, I enjoy effortless freestyle swimming. Every stroke is a bliss. Poetry in motion. I wonder can we possibly draw parallels between swimming and presentation?

Lessons in academic presentations

A quick glance, swimming and presentation are both skill- and performance-based pursuit; both require years of training to perfect the art. Upon reflection, I notice the following similarities:

- **Clear your mind.** Swimming with a mind full of things at work wouldn't be that enjoyable. One would hardly be engaged with each stroke; the feeling of oneness with water diminishes... Before I jump into the pool, I make sure I clear my mind of the day's matters. It allows me to become more aware of how each stroke and breathing feels. I am present.

- **Start with the end in mind.** I often start my swims with an aim e.g. to swim 10+10 (slow+fast) laps this session. Similarly, one of the first things I'd do is finding 3 key points or 1 message I want my audience to take home. Once I know my message, re-arranging ideas, concepts, principles etc into a story would be effortless. That's my creative process in a gist.

- **Mindful of yourself and your audience.** How I feel in water matters as it indicates 'my swimming shape'. As soon as I feel slow or 'draggy', I'd correct my form by straightening up my posture/head a little bit– so that my body is in one straight line from head to toe.

Always aim for the feeling of gliding in water. Like a dolphin. Similarly, always be aware of how you feel as you present ideas, concepts and facts. Look out for the audience's reactions as you speak.

- **Speak from your centre.** When you are aware and being authentic, you speak from your centre. You speak from your 'power station'. From this station, everything will fall into place, you are in the flow. Your presentation will feel light and effortless.

"Your life becomes a masterpiece when you learn to master peace."– JustDeen Things@Instagram

Empty Your Cup

One of my favourite stories is about the Professor and the tea cup. The story comes in many versions; one version of the story goes like this,

Nan-in, a Japanese master during the Meiji era, received a university professor who came to inquire about Zen.

Nan-in served tea. He poured his visitor's cup full, and then kept on pouring. The professor watched the overflow until he no longer could restrain himself. "It is overfull. No more will go in!"

Like this cup, Nan-in said, you are full of your own opinions and speculations. How can I show you Zen unless you first empty your cup?

• • •

The best way to communicate, in my opinion, is to listen first. If I am full of myself, I won't listen or even hear you. Because there are a lot of 'mental busy-ness' that block out information coming to your senses.

The mental busy-ness further serve as filters to your senses. You won't get the full picture. You only see what you want to see, hear what you want to hear. You are absent in the presence of the other person.

When I am nothing, I have no agenda. I am with you.
When I am nothing, my cup is empty. I am ready to receive you.
You may pour into me fully.

Lessons in academic presentations

- **Be present.** This is when magic happens. The presenter would be in oneness with the audience—on 'the same wavelength'. The presenter is in 'the flow'. The audience can tell. Time flies. It feels good.
- **Let go.** I find that, letting go of any pre-conceived ideas before coming into a workshop, helps me as a trainer when dealing with nervousness and jittery. It would be hard at first but gets much easier as time goes by. Learn to let go. Learn to empty your cup. Then, listen deeply.

"Knowledge is learning something every day. Wisdom is letting something go every day."
–Zen Proverb

From a CEO office

"People pay for space"–a point I make at my presentation workshop, and added, "the bigger the space, the more you pay. Take a CEO office for example."

Slides are spaces where words, visuals and shapes occupy the spaces. Like a spacious CEO office, the bigger space you give to those elements, the more power you confer to the message.

Besides that, a CEO office resides exclusively at the top of a hierarchy of an organisation. Design your important content and messages to reflect the exclusivity and spaciousness of a CEO office. With such clarity and focus, it delivers the greatest impact to your audience.

Data dumping, on the contrary, has undesirable effects. View it as an enemy who opposes to what you, as a presenter, aim for. Data dumping leads to sensory and cognitive overload, obstructs and confuses the very people you wish to influence and persuade.

To illustrate the invisible power of design, we can use a 2-dimensional (2D) photo of a Japanese Zen Garden as an example. A typical Japanese garden would have a circle or a figure-8 shape in the middle of pebbles of nothingness. Towards the edges of the garden there would be some shrubs of different heights—low, medium—in the foreground; the background of the edges are some plants—again of various shapes and heights.

Slides are spaces where words, visuals and shapes occupy... Like a spacious CEO office, the bigger space you give to those elements, the more power you confer to the message.

A Japanese Garden exemplifies the use of space and hierarchy in visual composition and landscape. Each has its own role in the whole composition. Individual element gracefully works together leading the eye from the anchor (a circle or a figure-8) to the little shrubs where the eye moves from the small one to the middle shrub and then on to the higher trees.

Here the eyes could rest and explore the visual textures and colours of trees. Thoughtful use of space and elements give rise to visual orderliness, and the feelings of calmness and serenity. There is so much one can learn about design from a Japanese garden.

For powerful presentation designs, take your cue from a CEO office.

Lessons in academic presentations

The world is a busy place. The competition for an audience's attention and focus has never been so fierce.

- Having basic knowledge in simple visual design helps a presenter to grab the attention of the audience to focus on his or her message.
- A well-designed slide deck is, in essence, intelligent use of spaces and elements to keep your audience focused.
- A less distracted audience makes a presenter's job much easier.
- Design supports, enhances and drives your message in an elegant manner to your audience–they may well be grant evaluators, Professors, colleagues and students.

"Design is not about products, design is about relationships."
–Hella Jongerius,
a Dutch industrial designer.

Creativity, Then and Now

A key skill in designing a presentation is how to convert text to visuals. Back then, the process of looking for the right images is tedious and can get extremely tiring. Especially when no image available to match the ones I have in mind.

To look for an exact image that comes to mind, I used to spend 1-2 hours meticulously combing stock photo sites. Therefore, for a typical slide deck of 30-40 slides, I would spend between 2-3 weeks preparing them.

One of the best investments I did was learning how to do a proper sketch using Adobe Illustrator.

Going through this creative process reminds me the words of Robin Sharma, "All change is hard at first, messy in the middle and gorgeous at the end."

I don't want to sound like tooting my own horn, but to be honest, this conversion comes to me naturally. When I read a text—scientific articles or textbook—many images come to me. They are like streams of visitors to my mind.

They would keep coming until I place them on my slides. Once done, I am happy.

The process of converting text with the right images feels natural and therapeutic to me. I also learned to use photo editing software. One of the best investments I did was learning how to do a proper sketch using Adobe Illustrator. That was 10 years ago.

"All change is hard at first, messy in the middle and gorgeous at the end."–Robin Sharma

Today, using mobile devices, ideas can be easily sketched and captured on the go, then transfer into a presentation app e.g. Powerpoint and Keynote. Much of my work nowadays consists of digital asset and using online apps to convert ideas to visuals.

Lessons in academic presentations

Learn to turn complex fact and data into simple visuals or sketches and infographics. Effectively, you make your content simpler and easier for your audience to understand. Great apps to create an infographic are Piktochart and Visme.

Doctor, I'm Not Creative

This is one of the most frequent comments I heard from my presentation workshop participants. I am intrigued as well, to be honest. I've shared my own creative processes in the previous story, but I always wonder how others do it? So I made it as one of my little quests to ask well-known or established performers, artists, writers and cartoonists how they continue to be creative and productive.

Several years ago, my friends and I had a wonderful opportunity of visiting Datuk Muhammad Nor Khalid at his home in Ipoh, Perak. Better known as Lat, Malaysia's renowned cartoonist, his cartoons are humorous and perfectly captured the many walks of life in Malaysia. He and his wife welcomed us into their home and instantly made us feel comfortable with funny and heart-warming stories of his career drawing cartoons. At some point, I asked him a question: Datuk, you're a prolific cartoonist. How do you continue to be creative? How do you get the ideas drawing cartoons?

With a twinkle in his eyes, he answered that he got his ideas for cartoons from the everyday things and events. From the news, conversations happening around him. Thank you Datuk for sharing the insight.

Perhaps many wonderful creative ideas are literally in front of us, waiting to be seen as they are. Not as we are.

Doctor, what's the best presentation software?

Or did you use Powerpoint? Top two questions I always get after my presentations. And I would get a disappointed look when my reply was, "Afraid not..."

I intentionally keep this story towards the end of this section. Because an effective presentation is more about sharing your message in the form of a story that moves an audience from point A to B. To where you want them to be. A presentation app is a tool that facilitates you, the presenter, to tell the story. To educate. To persuade. To leave a lasting impact on the audience.

...a competent (presentation app) user lends an aura of confidence when presenting their story.

In the 21st century, somehow, one tends to use a presentation app. Incompetency in using a presentation app often invites anxiety and nervousness in a speaker. When technical glitches occur, many inexperienced speakers get panicked, eyes desperately look for help and later unable to regain their composure. A few could even forget their speech.

On the other hand, a competent user lends an aura of confidence when presenting their story. Inevitably, members of the audience assume that a good speaker uses a special presentation app–a magic wand that casts a spell on the audience.

Each (presentation app) would have the pros and cons. The pros should support your needs and wants; the cons shouldn't restrict or put your pitch in jeopardy.

Looking for the presentation magic wand is a journey on its own. There is this habit of mine that would scour for any new presentation tool. I am always on the lookout for a tool that supports and lets me explore the creative (and uncreative) side of me. But I have to confess I don't have the best one. Yet.

Mainly because those questions beg you to identify your needs and wants. But when you're tired of Powerpoint... and seeking for alternatives. First of all, decide if you want to present offline or online. For offline options, you have Powerpoint, Canva, Haiku Deck, Prezi and Keynote.

Then, if you wish for an online presentation software that gives you fresh designs, stylish and super easy–sign up for Canva. For something dramatic and engaging, try Emaze as an online presentation tool. The downside is it's a data guzzler.

If you have plenty of graphs and diagrams to present, Piktochart could be your answer. And Prezi, it would be great for afternoon'ish presentation. When designed properly, you can craft a Prezi that dazzles your audience and keeps them wide-awake.

Not all presentations are created equal...

However, when you have explored the tools above, you would soon realise what it can do and what it can't do. Each would have the pros and cons. The pros should support your needs and wants; the cons shouldn't restrict or put your pitch in jeopardy.

The way I see it, not all presentations are created equal. Or for the same purpose. A presentation created for a keynote talk should be designed differently from a lecture. A presentation for a workshop differ in many ways than a research seminar. To this end, I have several go-to-apps that work for different purposes.

For instance, I prefer Sway for my workshop on presentation. I think it is particularly useful for educators, researchers and students who have some content and stories. Sway lets you focus on the content first, then delivers beautifully designed presentations in no time through artificial intelligence.

My favourite app for teaching and Interactive Lecture workshops used to be Blendspace. Chiefly because I loved to 'drag and drop' multimedia contents e.g. videos, pdf, Powerpoint into the empty boxes. Then, share the Blendspace link with my students. All the learning materials are in one place; they can watch a video, review a Powerpoint and read a pdf without having to open them in separate windows. Plus, it's available as an iPad app. So convenient and versatile.

At number 2 and 3...

Ranked at number 2 and 3, respectively, are Canva and Piktochart. I design my presentations using these two tools when I want something fresh, eye-catching and contemporary for my audiences.

Watch this video presentation at Taylor's Teaching and Learning conference 2018, http://bit.ly/18ttlc. The presentation was created using a Canva template. A 16-minute presentation. The template has a nice light green and grey design. It's easy on the eye.

Because I had some research data and photos, it took about 1 hour plus to design this preso. I then spent another 30-40 minutes to create the video presentation using Screencastify. The design and video recording took place in a hotel room somewhere near KLCC. Right after that I needed to go to IUCEL in IIUM.

Thus, the great things about Canva and Piktochart are that these presentation software provide well-designed templates. Just point and click. Add content. And you are good to go. Or share with others on social media.

They serve a purpose.

And the top spot goes to...

For presentation design, reigning at the top spot is Apple Keynote. I've been using it since I bought my first Mac Book. It was a present to self. Since then, I haven't looked back to PC.

Most of my teaching slides are designed using Keynote. The sample slide deck featured in the classic presentation book, Presentation Zen i.e. 'Aromatic Chemistry' slides were designed and delivered using this app.

Additionally, I designed my entire 'ACE That Presentation' MOOC in Keynote–from the slide deck designs, logo, thumbnails, colour scheme, font family. It's a 4-month DIY effort–day in, day out, several times in the weekends. A distillation of 13-year experience in presentation design and delivery in higher education–all can be learned in 4 weeks or less.

In sum, I found Keynote so simple and intuitive to use. It provides the space for unleashing my creativity. It's powerful. And it's great for non-designers.

My magic wand.

The Tale of Two Presenters

The first presenter comes in with high energy. He walks all over the room as he talks. He keeps on talking, talking and talking. He hardly takes a pause. After a morning break, he continues talking about his work with his students. How he designs classroom activities, how wonderful his students are, what are the pitfalls to avoid during designing such activities.

"Sharing knowledge is not about giving people something, or getting something from them. That is only valid for information sharing. Sharing knowledge occurs when people are genuinely interested in helping one another develop new capacities for action; it is about creating learning processes."–Peter Senge

He invites 2-3 questions from the participants. But just questions, he seems less interested in learning about the other person's experiences nor allows the questioner to speak longer than himself.

The first half-hour into the session, participants seem to be attentive and listen to his talk. Nonetheless, when the talk continues non-stop, it causes many participants to switch off. Instead, the participants can be seen to be working on their computers and chit chat with each other. They no longer seem to want to participate in the incessant monologue of Mr 'Know-It-All'.

This takes place at a national workshop. Most participants are heads of department, coordinators or leading educators in the field. They let out a big sigh of relief when lunch is announced. A participant said, "Let's pray the afternoon speaker won't be like him."

The afternoon speaker

The second speaker starts his session promptly at 2.30 pm. A soft-spoken and articulate presenter, he gives a short introduction about himself and what he aims to do in 2 hours. This is followed by an activity using Padlet. "Let's get to know one another," he says.

Everyone gets to participate and contribute in the activities. Everyone learns insights from one another.

He shares the Padlet link and waits for responses from participants. There is a buzz of activities in the room. After 10 minutes or so, he looks through the responses on the Padlet wall. He calls out the names of the participants, asking where they are coming from. Participants look for persons who names are being called out. Who is that? She is the Dr. XYZ from university of so and so. Ohhh... I've heard her names so many times. Now I can put a name to the person, and so on. This ice-breaking activity creates loud buzzes around the room.

In a short time, he taps into the vast experiences of the participants and facilitate meaningful discussions. Great lessons on constructivism and adult learning.

Soon after that activity, he gives another activity–a longer one that requires group discussions. "I'm sharing a scenario here, it's called the tale of two classrooms. Can you all discuss amongst yourselves at a table? Then share which classroom you prefer to be in and why? You guys have 15 minutes, share your thoughts on the same Padlet."

The silence is broken by noises that grow louder and louder over time. It buzzes with lively discussions, arguments and laughters. Participants are so into the activity—one activity after another. Soon, the afternoon session comes to an end.

Everyone gets to take part and contribute in the activities. Everyone learns insights from one another. Sharing and communication are facilitated by technology. Because of these, everyone seems energised and happier during the afternoon session. Time flies so fast.

In contrast to the first presenter, the second presenter learns from the participants. He creates the space for the participants to get to know each other. He creates the right environment that encourages people to discuss and collaborate. He listens to them. He empowers the participants to find their voice as individuals and as a group. In a short time, he taps into the vast experiences of the participants and facilitate meaningful discussions. Great lessons on constructivism and adult learning.

A huge departure from the first presenter who later reluctantly admits that he has a lot to learn from the second presenter.

Such is the tale of two presenters. Which presenter do you wish to be?

2. Teaching

Earn Your Space

I asked my students how did they find my lectures? And quickly added, you know you can be honest with me. One of them replied it's interesting so far, it's not boring. And why is that? I further inquired. The student and her friends replied, "because Doctor, you moved a lot during lectures."

During lectures, I like to move from one end of the lecture hall to the other while addressing big groups of students. I would climb the steps, stop in the middle and talk to those sitting on the sides. If no bags or things blocking my path, I would walk across the lecture hall, randomly stop at any students and ask simple questions. I probed their thinking. That stirred some excitements in my students. They laughed at their own thinking. Great!

I asked them how they arrived at their answers. I listened carefully. To me, it matters less if the answer is right or wrong. An answer is a destination. Walk, take a bus, a train or fly to a destination. Often, those who arrive quickest at the correct answer may have some alternative thinking and way of doing things.

Rather than the destinations, I am more interested in the journey (of the minds and hearts). In time, when the psychological barriers between students and educators are pulled down, I find my students smart and creative—they can do amazing things that never ever cross my mind.

In higher education, what also matters is that students are willing to learn from mistakes, able to rationalise the why and adjust their thinking accordingly. And go on teaching others. Spread the knowledge, analogous to a river that runs its course to refresh, purify and nourish others.

Simply by not fixing myself to the one spot—the front of the lecture hall, behind a computer—during my lectures creates unique learning and bonding moments with my students. In that briefest moments, I showed how much I care about their learning. I learned and unlearned with them, and I earned the space in their hearts.

Lessons in academic presentations

Interact with students, conference or workshop participants—before, during and after your presentations or lectures. Plan, design and allocate time for such activities, where a two-way communication is encouraged and sustained throughout the session. This is when one builds a firm foundation for more amazing learning and teaching moments in academic life.

Carpe diem!

Drawing from the heart

I'm sharing a diagram of an action potential from heart muscles drawn in Keynote as shown below. Keynote has a line tool that you can further manipulate into shapes. Or you can modify any shapes or icons in Keynote to your liking. It took about 20 minutes to create the following diagram (low resolution shown) for my presentation.

Then, I numbered the phases of this action potential from 4 – 0 – 1 – 4. Like Canva, Keynote provides a great selection of nice fonts for professional use–something I often share in my presentation workshops. Careful selection of certain fonts, e.g. a change from Times New Roman to Helvetica Neue (light) will help invigorate your dull presentation.

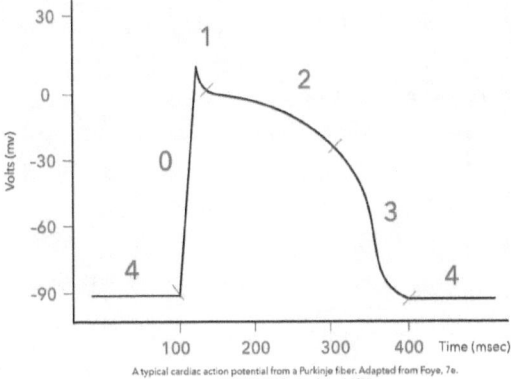

A typical cardiac action potential from a Purkinje fiber. Adapted from Foye, 7e.
CC BY-NC-ND, Dr. Aisyah Saad, 2018

In less 300 microseconds, many events occur during these phases 4 – 0 – 1 – 4. Phase 4 is a resting potential for myocardiac tissues, 0 represents depolarisation and 1 – 3 are re-polarisation phases. The important ones are the influx and efflux of salts, sodium, potassium and calcium. These salts are critical for the pumping action of the heart.

And that is why we need to keep an eye on our dietary salts. Too little or too much could affect our heart, blood circulation and overall well-being.

Coming back to the diagram, there is a huge amount of information to teach my undergraduate pharmacy students. Quite a lot to digest for them. But if I follow one of my dad's acetate tips, that is to present the large amount of information bit-by-bit, phase-by-phase, then it should work. I presented these sequence of events to my students as it happens in the heart. From my heart to theirs.

"The desire to create is one of the deepest yearnings of the human soul."–Dieter Uchtdorf

Power Pauses

Use pauses strategically during your lecture session. At the start of a class, it tends to be noisy, with lots of movements—papers tussles, bags and tumblers crash and hit each other, students joking about. Instead of starting with a hello or a shout to cut through the noise, try to a power pause.

What do I mean with 'power pause'? Stand in front of the audience, shoulders square, both feet firmly on the ground and look at them. Don't stare or give a killer look. Simply give a gentle look, hop from one face to the next. If the room is big (a lecture hall of over 100 people), divide the room into a quadrant. Look at 1-2 faces in one quadrant, then move your attention to the next one. Do this in silence.

...when you stand in front and remain quiet, your audience will tune in their energy to yours.

Keep doing this exercise until the noise has died down. You may take 30 seconds or even 1-2 minutes... You might initially find it nerve-wrecking since our natural inclination is to avoid an awkward silence. Besides, it might be quite uncomfortable to have all eyes on you.

To reduce the uneasy feelings, turn your inner focus to listening to the surrounding while maintaining the gentle look. Or feel how your feet feel against the floor. Or listen to your heartbeats.

And when do I know they start to pay attention to me? When the stillness feels so thick and heavy that you can hear a pin drop. Now they are ready to listen to your lecture.

Why this happens? Because non-verbal language speaks louder than verbal. Most times, 3 times louder and more effective than saying things out to control a room. Whether they are your students, fellow researchers, Professors–your audience's energy will follow the leader. So when you stand in front and remain quiet, your audience will tune in their energy to yours.

"The right word may be effective, but no word was ever as effective as a rightly timed pause."–Mark Twain.

Power pauses can also be applied in the middle of a lecture. Or design a lecture by introducing power pauses in the beginning, middle and end. A pause can be from 5 seconds to 1-2 minute. Posing a simple question to your audience will turn a quiet pause into an interactive intermission.

Strategic use of power pauses works well in keynote speeches, particularly a speaker wishes to place emphasis on certain words or concepts.

Introducing a pause towards the end of a presentation gives your audience an opportunity to reflect. For instance, you can guide your audience by asking them to take 1 minute to think about what they have learned from your session. Having an uninterrupted time for reflection improves a person's chance to connect their prior knowledge with what you present. It improves understanding, promotes deeper learning and allows the space for further insights.

The former US President Barack Obama is the Master of Pause. Strategic use of power pauses works well in keynote speeches, particularly a speaker wishes to place emphasis on certain words or concepts. It lends gravity and re-frames an audience's attention to what's coming next. Leave them with a lasting impression using power pauses.

The Magic Number 3

Times have changed. Our daily life is inundated with news, social media, blog that scream for our attention, every second of the day. It is not difficult to get drowned in all these things happening around us.

In the current higher education scenarios, I suggest you design your presentation by taking into account short attention span. As mentioned in earlier, one way is to introduce pauses in a 50-minute lecture.

In 1956, a cognitive psychologist from Princeton University, George A. Miller put forward a theory on human capacity for short-term memory. This theory became known as 'Miller's Magical Number 7 Theory'. Our working memory has an upper limit of processing and remembering information at any given time.

Presenting chunks of information or data help the learning process.

Seven plus/minus two seems to be the magical number, Miller discovered. The items may consist of digits, words, letters or units. The current trend in presentations tend to favour the rule of three. Some examples of the magic number 3:

- Beginning, Middle and End: a three-part story.
- "Stop-Look-Listen": road safety campaigns for children.
- "The World of Three Zeros": the title of the talk by Prof. Muhammad Yunus.

What are the implications of Miller's Magical Number 7 to presentations in higher education? Being aware of Miller's Magical Number 7 can help us design presentations that minimise information overloading to our audiences.

Chunk large information into smaller groups. Identify 3-7 similar items and group them together. Presenting chunks of information or data help the learning process. It can lead to better retention and understanding of what you share during your presentation.

Lessons in academic presentations

Apple seems obsessed with the rule of three. For instance, three colours, three sizes of iPhones. If you want your audience to remember your work, simplify and chunk information or knowledge into three. Or at best, one.

Be succinct. The rest you can give away as infographics, documents and articles.

Interactive Lecture

A typical lecture slot is 50 minutes. When I started my job as a lecturer, I used to think that I needed to cover the syllabus for the courses I teach in 50 minutes. Because everyone (my colleagues) around me were doing the same thing. I used to think that my students' minds are like big vessels or sponges that soak in information effortlessly. And I used to think teaching is uni-directional, from me to them. A sage on the stage.

That students had no role during lectures. They were simply passive recipients of the knowledge. They were supposed to keep quiet and listen to me. Just like my undergraduate days.

Huge mistakes. Thanks to the training I received in teaching and learning workshops, together with numerous discussions with fellow educators, I learned to be a better educator. Or rather, in time, I was able to unlearn the above erroneous thinking and practices.

Interactive lecture is one of the teaching strategies that has transformed my lectures.

I learned that teaching is a two-way street. I learned about active learning and designing simple activities to support active learning in students.

Students, in today's higher education, are those born in 1997 onwards. The digital natives, Gen-alpha and younger. These generations play, learn and work differently than my generation. Where passivity is perhaps expected (and well-accepted) during my time, I learned that my students respond better to active learning activities.

> *"If we teach today's students as we taught yesterday's, we rob them of tomorrow."–Dewey*

I realised learning happens when students start to talk, argue, agree/disagree and share their thoughts. Learning happens when they are able to make mistakes and learning from their mistakes in a safe environment. I learned to create a safe environment to support and promote active learning during lectures.

Interactive lecture is one of the teaching strategies that has transformed my lectures. Using the rule of three, as mentioned earlier, you can chunk a 50-minute presentation session into 3 lecturettes of 10-15 minutes. Preferably 10 minutes, followed by short bursts of activities.

A typical interactive lecture plan:
- Divide into 3 segments of 15-minute lecturettes.
- Each lecturette is followed by a pause of 30 seconds to 3 minutes. This pause can simple be a space to allow your students to catch up with their own thoughts and re-center themselves for the next lecturette.
- In the next pause, you can do a short activity called 'Think-Pair-Share'. This activity is also known as an 'engagement trigger'. Throw a question, ask students to think on their own, pair with neighbours to discuss their thoughts, then share with the entire class. Consider their answers and adjust your lecture accordingly. This activity takes about 2-3 minutes.
- Continue with the third lecturette that ends with a 1-minute reflection, for instance 'what are 3 things you have learned in this lecture' and/or ask for feedback.
- Study the reflections. Rinse and repeat the lecture plan in the next lecture.
- Adjust your teaching strategies according to the reflection and/or feedback you have received from your students.
- Scrutinise the topic or concepts that your students find the most challenging in the next lecture. Think of an activity to clarify the concepts or applications to students.

There are many activities to make a lecture more interactive, e.g. fishbowl, mind mapping, crossword puzzles. I find interactive lecture strategies great in capturing and sustaining attention in a large class—it works wonders in afternoon classes.

I no longer cover syllabus; instead I design lecture time to let my students learn through discovery and play. Yes, it takes some effort and time to implement this, but the best part of this interactive lecture approach? I get to learn from my students and improve my teaching practices.

You can do a short activity called 'Think-Pair-Share'. This activity is also known as an 'engagement trigger'. Throw a question, ask students to think on their own, pair with (their) neighbours to discuss their thoughts, then share with the entire class.

Doctor, can I have your slides?

Nowadays, sharing a presentation slide deck with students and participants, after a talk, seems to be a common practice. Somehow it is expected of a presenter to share his or her powerpoint. Some participants even bring along their thumb drives, ready to copy the slides. And the reluctance to share your powerpoint suddenly makes you feel like a bad guy. So... to share or not to share?

Sharing has become a significant characteristic in this digital age. Take for instance, listening to songs. Back in 2001, when iPod was introduced, Steve Jobs' catchy marketing tagline is "1000 songs in your pocket." That clever tagline underlines the amount of hard disk storage an MP3 player offers.

Fast forward to today, one no longer owns songs, albums or pay subscriptions to a channel, instead one simply shares a playlist of 1000 songs. Or a million in your pocket. Endless listening, for as long you wish, as long as you are connected. The rise of Youtube, Spotify...

I believe whether to share comes down to 1) your own personal and 2) professional preferences. Sure, when one spends time long enough in academic circles, one has heard plenty of academic horror stories on intellectual property infringements. The profits of such infringements are abundant in the world of key performance index (KPIs). Protecting one's intellectual property is advisable, and the following are some suggestions:

Second copy. I learned this tip from one of my postdoctoral researchers. Present your 'master copy' during the seminar, but be ready with an abbreviated version of your presentation. Give this second copy away, if asked. Or if you feel a little reluctant, upload your presentation on Slideshare and share the link.

Online presentations. Fully online presentation apps, such as Blendspace or Prezi (free version), allow embeds of multimedia e.g. Youtube videos, online pdfs. Use this feature in your presentations. This way you are sharing what are already out there on other platforms.

Creative commons or copyright. If you wish to share your presentation with the world, you can also protect your work under Creative Commons (CC) licences: https://creativecommons.org/ Several licences are available, from a flexible (CC BY) to the most restricted (CC BY-NC-ND). In all CC licences, a user needs to cite the creator of the work without seeking prior permission when sharing the work with others. To use copyrighted materials, as you are aware, the permission needs to be sought, prior to sharing. Whether to go for a CC or copyright protection depends on your ultimate aim and comfort level in terms of sharing your intellectual work.

Presenting to Win

"What are those colourful things in the bags?" a lecturer from School of Mass Communications asked. Dr. J, she introduced herself.

"Oh these?... They are balloons," came my reply. I was a nervous-wreck. Pacing around the huge waiting room as we saw judges, one by one, arrived and walked into the Vice-Chancellor meeting room. Except for 2-3 familiar faces of the university's Deputy Vice Chancellor and Professors, the rest of judges looked so unfamiliar. There was even a young man, who looks like a student. Who are these people? I was thinking and trying to remember the faces...

Dr. J broke my train of thoughts when she asked, "What are the balloons for?..."

"They are for the microteaching session," I replied, then asked, "What do you bring?"

"Just my Powerpoint," replied Dr. J in perfect English and gave a confident smile.

(Oh wow... I thought I'm not sure if I could just win this award with just a Powerpoint)

At that moment, the third lecturer walked in carrying two huge shopping bags. He sat down and took out two massively thick D-ring folders, each as thick as 2 bricks, from the shopping bags. The Secretariat introduced him to us, "This is Dr. M, from our Engineering campus."

Vying for Teaching Excellence Award
We had been nominated for the university's Teaching Excellence Award (Anugerah Pendidik Sanjungan, APS). In previous years, winners were selected according to clusters e.g. Applied Sciences, Health Sciences, Social Sciences and so on. Each cluster had one winner. That year, however, due to budget constraints, the APS committee would select one overall winner for the university teaching award.

He then asked me, "So, what do you bring for the microteaching session?" I replied, "Just those balloons," and pointed to a bagful of balloons by the sofa.

I was struck by how thick both folders were. After short introductions, I asked Dr. M, "What are those for?..." He replied, "These folders are my teaching evidence for the award."

"Wow... That's a lot of evidence!" I exclaimed.

Dr. M broke into the biggest grin when he saw my surprised face. He then asked me, "So, what do you bring for the microteaching session?"

I replied, "Just those balloons," and pointed to a bagful of balloons by the sofa. I could see Dr. M hadn't stopped grinning with a twinkle in his eyes. Perhaps, he just realised what a huge advantage he was having towards winning the award—two monster thick folders, full of teaching evidence versus some colourful balloons, full of air.

The head judge came out and briefed us about the judging process. Dr. M would go in first, followed by me and Dr. J. We wished each other good luck.

• • •

I could hear Dr. M giving a lecture to the panel. Quite a powerful voice. Then, came the clapping. I guess that's the end of his sessions. "Next is my turn," I said to myself, "remember your plan."

Dr. M came out with those two thick folders, flashing another confident grin. All the best, he said to me. "Thank you, I need that," I replied and trying to shake off my nervousness.

I walked in, setup my Mac and waited for the cue to start. In the semi-dark meeting room, I managed to see 10 judges sitting in a semi-circle formation. I could make out perhaps 3 familiar faces, the rest were unknown. The judges were seated at one end of the long meeting room, and I was on the other.

I thought, "Hmmm... My voice is not the loudest. It's perhaps best for me to go closer to them."

The microteaching session

The head judge then greeted me, and gave the 'permission' to me to treat them like my own students.

"You may start now."

The moment of truth.

I opened my presentation with a question,"Who has had a tooth infection before?"

Some of my "students" raised their hands. "What did you have to treat the infection?"

"Amoxicillin", "ampicillin..." my "students" responded.

"Goooood... do you know that those belong to the antibiotic, penicillins?" I said.

They nodded in unison.

By the end of this lecture, you will have a huge structure of penicillin in your hands!

"Okay, so today we are going to learn about penicillin, how they were discovered, how penicillin kill bacteria. You will learn about penicillin structure, how it is closely related to its action. Not only that, by the end of this lecture, you will have a huge structure of penicillin in your hands!"

As planned, I proceeded with a 10-minute lecture on the discovery, chemistry and action of penicillin. Banking on the power of visuals, I illustrated my points using images with just the right amount of text. I didn't want to crowd the slide deck with text.

I reasoned that my "students" were from different disciplines. I kept my slide simple and straightforward. I wanted to make complex subject on antimicrobial therapy accessible and easily understood by anyone. I used lots of analogies, durians and rambutans included, to show how bacteria looked like, and how penicillins work causing the death of bacteria.

Huge penicillin structure in your hand
Ten minutes into the presentation, I asked my "students" do you know how penicillin look like? They shook their heads. At that point, I asked my assistant to bring in the balloons.

They laughed, squealed with delight as they were twisting the balloons. A couple of balloons burst, and they cried out loud for new balloons.

As the balloons were being distributed around the meeting room, I could see my "students" were getting a little excited. They started playing and waving the balloons to each other. Some even wanted to choose the colour of the balloons. They waited impatiently for my next instruction... Hahaha... Balloons brought out the inner child in them.

I drew their attention back to the lesson at hand, "Okay, let's build a structure of penicillin using the balloons. We will do it in 3 steps." As I took them step-by-step–twisting the balloons at certain points like a sausage and tying to the other end to form a ring.

Though the meeting room was quite dark, I thought I could see twinkles in their eyes.

They laughed, squealed with delight as they were twisting the balloons. A couple of balloons burst, and they cried out loud for new balloons. It was quite noisy as they were teaching each other and joked around. "Great," I said to myself, "... they seem to enjoy playing and hopefully learning something from this lesson."

By the end of the activity, everyone had a huge (partial) structure of penicillin in their hand, on the table (a couple on their heads!). Everyone was smiling. Some "students" i.e. Professors were seen admiring their balloon handiwork. Though the meeting room was quite dark, I thought I could see twinkles in their eyes.

At that point, I thought I could finish off the microteaching session with the chemistry of penicillin.

Before I could open my mouth, I was stopped by a judge. "Time's up!" he said sternly,"...let's proceed with the Q&A session."

A week later, an official letter arrived in my pigeon hole. I won!

Lessons in academic presentations

This experience cemented the ways I approach a presentation. I learned to:
- keep my lecture sweet and simple, tailored to my audience who come from various disciplines.
- use the rule of three. Three big ideas. Three steps.
- mix things up: opened with questions, use of images and colours in the short lecture, followed by a fun activity.
- include elements of unexpectedness and fun in my presentation. My "students" didn't expect to play and learn to construct penicillin rings with balloons!

Remember My Name

The lyrics of the Fame song by Irene Clara:

"Baby, look at me
And tell me what you see
You ain't seen the best of me yet
Give me time
I'll make you forget the rest
I got more in me
And you can set it free
I can catch the moon in my hand
Don't you know who I am

Remember my name, fame
I'm gonna live forever
I'm gonna learn how to fly, high"...

This song captures the essence of an educator's role, to see the potential in your students, to awaken and nurture the soul, the spirit and then sets it free to roam the world.

If there is one thing I wish you have as a takeaway from this section is to remember the names of your students. When you present, call out the names. It has the magical power of touching lives, and as Steve Jobs puts it, "make a dent in (their) universe."

3. Grants and Research

Harness first impressions

As much as we wish to deny the tendency that we judge a book by its cover, it is true to some extent. And the first impression matters as the saying goes.

The title is our audience's first impression of us. It provides an idea of what's coming in your talk. So what is the secret to a good cover slide? Think of a catchy or provocative title yet quite specific. A Twitter-like title is a good length. Couple it with interesting visuals related to the topic.

For instance, a title on 'Basic Research in Thermodynamics' can be re-phrased to something interesting e.g. 'Harnessing energy systems in the 21st century' or 'Unlocking the Secrets of Ancient Civilisations through Lessons in Thermodynamics'. Tie a topic to possible applications could elicit interests from your students or audience.

A Twitter-like title is a good length.

Seeing the catchy and visually captivating slide cover could attract and make your audience stay and listen to your talk. Next, they would ask themselves:

- What's in for me? (WIIFM)
- Is it worth of my time?
- Is there something else better on Youtube than this presentation or lecture?

To address the above questions, give an outline of your talk and state 3 points or benefits of listening to your talk. In my opinion, this is one of the most crucial moments in any presentation. Hook your audience before going into the main part of your presentation.

One common mistake I've seen in many academic presentation is when one treats a presentation like a written publication.

Slides after slides are full of text, leaving little room for visual. Or the visuals are too small–"just as a decoration"– I heard an educator put it. Bullet points are added to 'aid' audience and presenter while reading the slide.

What's in for me?
Is it worth of my time?

A text-laden presentation turns a "powerful" presentation into "powerless" presentation. Text strips away the power from the presenter and puts the power into the slides. Because your audience, while reading the text on slides, will pay less attention to you and what you are saying. Make it worthy for the audience.

Remember... we eat with our eyes.

We eat with our eyes

We can use visuals as signposts and anchors to direct an audience's attention and navigate their minds during your presentation. Let me share another secret with you.

We eat with our eyes *first*. Japanese are good at this. Servings of sushi and sashimi are always beautifully arranged in a manner that stimulate our appetite.

It's an art and science. An obsession, a pride that runs deep into oneself, their cultures and how they work as a society. To appreciate the supreme level of craftsmanship, watch 'Jiro Dreams of Sushi'. It's a wonderful documentary about Jiro Ono, a sushi master who owns a Michelin three-star restaurant Sukiyabashi Jiro.

My sister reminded me that this phrase came from my late dad. I remember now how he recounted his dining experience during his work visits to Japan. From stunningly beauty of Japanese cuisines to the elegant ikebana and the punctuality of the Japanese. By design.

Take the effort to turn an academic presentation into a well-crafted visual feast that is memorable to your audience–your students, grant panel or peers. Give them Instagrammable moments.

In the 21st century, harness the power of social media to present you and your work in the best light.

RM240,000 in 3 minutes

"In 3 minutes?" I asked in a surprised tone.

"Yes, the grant review panels want to hear why you need that amount of money. They are looking at other researches as well. There is a long queue and the extra funding is not so big. The panels need to be selective. So don't get your hopes too high… plus it's already 3 o'clock in the afternoon. A quick presentation is all that they want to hear from you," the Secretariat patiently explained to us outside the hotel meeting room.

I asked, "When is our turn?"

"After 2 more researchers have presented, it will be your turn, Doctor…" said the Secretariat.

My mind was racing. What should I tell them? What do they want to hear? My research had been ongoing for 1.5 years. Together with co-researchers, we realised our laboratory work was tedious and our progress was super slow. The bottleneck in drug discovery usually lies in drug synthesis.

We searched for ways to speed things up and realised that we could not go *via* the conventional ways. We learned that a microwave for organic synthesis could be the answer we were looking for.

Heating a frozen dish in a microwave is much quicker than on a stove. Similarly, synthesis of desired compounds can take place in seconds or minutes, rather than hours, under the right conditions in microwaves.

Since there is no such equipment in Malaysia, we needed to find out how good a microwave is for organic synthesis. While many claimed the use of microwave to speed up chemical reactions, the reported experiments were performed in household microwave. It was in 2009. Few laboratories in the world had the microwave for organic synthesis facility where the heating is consistent and designed for chemical reactions.

After several enquiries, we found that the closest laboratory with the microwave facility. There was one in the National University of Singapore (NUS). Under the grant, we went to a Nobel Laureate talk by Professor Suzuki at the A*STAR followed by a fruitful visit to the facility in NUS.

I planned to present only 3 slides in less than 3 minutes.

Convinced that purchasing a microwave could improve the speed of making compounds to fight Avian Flu, we enquired about the price. After a series of discussions, we decided to ask for RM240,000 to include consumables and research materials over the remaining research period.

It's a large amount of money. We were convinced, but how could I convince the panels in 3 minutes?

I came up with a plan. I planned to present only 3 slides in less than 3 minutes.

- The first slide listed the achievement of my research group so far.
- The second slide showed a picture of the microwave for organic synthesis.
- The third slide showed the projection—what we aim to achieve in the next 1.5 years.

All must align to the overarching expectation of the university research grant—funding for the Accelerated Programmes in Excellence (APEX). I remember Guy Kawasaki's words: "Simple and to the point is always the best way to get your point across." So I decided to keep things simple.

That would clearly tie in with the APEX mission, I thought.

Just as we were called into the meeting room, an idea popped up. Hastily, I typed in a one-sentence caption in the second slide, 'Accelerating synthesis of compounds for Avian Flu'. I placed it on the top part of the microwave photo. That would tie in with the APEX mission, I thought.

When our turn came, the project head presented first to the panels about the entire project. She took several minutes, so when my turn came, I had less than 3 minutes.

As planned, I presented the achievement of my research group, 1.5 years into the research. Moving on to the second slide, I remember saying, "Why we put forward this microwave is because as the APEX university we want to accelerate research. In the same vein, we want to accelerate the pace of making our compounds to combat Avian Flu. Synthesis of chemical compounds is slow and challenging. If the panels give us the funding to buy this machine, it will help accelerate our research." That was my pitch for RM240,000.

A few days later, the Secretariat informed us the results of the panel. We got it!

The additional RM240,000 to purchase the microwave. Later I heard that was the highest amount awarded. The rest of researchers received 10 - 20% of the amount.

Lessons in academic presentations

What I learned from this experience about grant presentations to a panel:
- Don't make people to think (too much). Just show and tell. Leverage on the power of simple visuals.
- Match what you want with the funding agency's mission.
- Keep things simple, if not simpler.

50 slides in 10 minutes

How many slides do you have? asked a colleague of mine. She was one of the plenary speakers at 4th KANITA International Conference on Gender Studies (KICGS) 2018. Together with my colleague, we would speak at 'Special MOOC Panel on Women's Empowerment through Technology' session.

I replied, "About 40. For a 10-minute presentation, I'd present like 2 seconds."

Later that evening I discovered it was 50.

Does it matter? Yes, it does because it is a 9-month work on design and development of an inter-institutional MOOC for single mothers. How does one present 50 slides in 10 minutes?

Often in a conference or a symposium, the time given for a panelist or speaker is 15+5 minutes. Fifteen minutes for a presentation and 5 minutes for Q&A. Or 20 minutes with 5 minutes of Q&A at the end of a session—questions directed to all panel members.

At this session, panelists were given 10 minutes each to share our work with the conference audience.

I had to think of a strategy. An idea came, present it like a PechaKucha, but with some differences. PechaKucha is a 20x20 presentation. Twenty slides, each for 20 seconds. Arising from the brainchild of two architect-friends who wanted to find a way to present their enormous work in a briefest time. It's been called 'the art of concise presentation'. And it's great for visual communication.

So I reasoned out that for a 10 minute presentation, presenting a slide for 20 seconds seems not unlike a PechaKucha. Since I didn't have the luxury of time. I decided to take this route. Presenting 50 slides in 10 minutes? Can a presentation be more concise than a PechaKucha? You do the maths...

With this realisation, I re-designed my slide deck with the following objectives in mind:

1) meet the given time,

2) suit the audience, and

3) what I want them to remember.

The session, though was delayed for 30 minutes - past lunchtime, went smoothly, attracted several questions from the floor and stayed within the scheduled time.

• • •

Upon reflection on this event, I would like to share several tips in helping you more intentional and strategic in delivering your presentations:

- **Less is more.** Identify 3 takeaways for your audience and work from there to plan your awesome talk.

- **Give a visual tour.** Under a time constraint, consider giving your audience a visual tour of a project or research. Consider presenting with images rather than text. Text takes longer to read as opposed to images.
- **Do a power pause at each point.** This helps your audience to remember your points.
- **Pace is critical**. On each takeaway for your audience, slow down at these points to emphasise the points or stories you wish to impart. Spend a longer time to draw your audience's attention to the details of an important takeaway. Then pick up the pace.

In short, sometimes you go fast; on important points you go slow. Mix the paces with text and images to make your presentation interesting, impactful and engaging (to distract the audience from thinking of lunch!).

"The mind is not a vessel to be filled, but a fire to be kindled."
–Plutarch, a Greek writer and philosopher.

Presentation from Hell

At a research seminar, Professor Z was invited to deliver a talk on the impact of the fourth industrial revolution (4IR) on education. Professor Z opened the talk highlighting the roles of machine learning and big data in education. In the talk, Professor Z also compared the traditional pathway in the universities and envisioned more flexible pathways of learning in the future. One that is characterised by the rise of numerous offerings of online courses–as MOOCs, modular courses and programmes.

As the talk continued, suddenly Professor Z switched the screen black. Everyone in the room turned to the speaker–puzzled, curious and awaited for what's next. Professor Z then said, "Do you know how I turn the screen black?" No, came the reply from the audience of academics, almost in unison. "Ha! If you don't know about this simple thing, how will you fare in the 4IR?" said Professor Z, who seemed to enjoy the entire game of 'I know more than you'. With a smirk, he then revealed, "You press the "B" key, like this…" he grinned.

He may have won the silly mind game, but lost the opportunity to capture the hearts of his audience. A great presenter and educator make people feel smart and inspiring them to learn more about the world.

4. Notes for Aspiring Researchers and Students

Winning sketches

I remember one outstanding presentation by a young research officer at Sarawak Biodiversity Centre. I was invited to the Centre for the second time as a panelist and a keynote speaker. He and his teammate had a big task at hand, to develop an entire system for the Centre. The bioinformatics and laboratory management system would connect various sections and people in the Centre.

From my experience, it is challenging to talk about a sophisticated system, without resorting to being technical, dry and confusing. How does one do a technical presentation to a panel of academics, without being too technical?

He arranged each sketch in an interesting progressive storyline. We were hooked.

In contrast to earlier presenters who used text and images, he used his own sketches in his presentation. He was confident and spoke clearly. He presented the 4W1H (why, what, when, who and how)–each as a sketch. He arranged each sketch in an interesting progressive storyline. We were hooked. And I couldn't stop smiling.

He told a story that informs the audience. Yet it was his simple sketches that amplified his message and won the panelist's hearts. He received the best presenter award.

• • •

I have seen and been to hundreds of presentations in my lifetime as an academic, but this young officer made a scientific presentation simple and effective with a touch of elegance. A lesson in simplicity and creativity using sketches in a presentation.

Thanks to Dan Roam and sketchnotes artists, sketching and cartoons have been widely accepted and used in many academic conferences. In several Massive Open Online Courses (MOOCs), academics present using cartoons and animations–a wonderful example is 'Exploring Bioethics through Manga' MOOC.

Lessons in academic presentations

- One doesn't need a sophisticated presentation app to design and deliver an impactful presentation.
- Learn to craft a memorable story from four basic storylines–drama, pitch, explanation and report–as described by Dan Roam.
- Use simple, legible sketches as a medium to support and illustrate your story.

A note from young researcher

I was invited to give an afternoon talk to postgraduate students at the Institute for Molecular Medicines (INFORMM), Universiti Sains Malaysia (USM). In the beginning, I was unsure on how to proceed. The assistant registrar suggested a working title "How to give a good research presentation."

Over a phone conversation, I shared my predicaments with her, "For some time, I've been conducting a full day presentation workshop to educators. In contrast, this proposed workshop is targeted to a younger crowd. Furthermore, you are asking me to deliver it at half the amount of time of a typical workshop. There are so many to share. What you are requesting seems quite challenging," I said.

Eventually, I said yes to the officer, hung up and started re-thinking the design of the current workshop. How can I deliver a short but impactful workshop to young researchers? What are really important to them? What are 3 takeaways I want them to gain from my workshop? I keep asking myself these questions.

Decided to share 3 most erroneous assumptions and mistakes ... in the academic world, and how to overcome them.

I reflected upon my Ph.D. days. Going down the memory lane. I dug deep and decided to share 3 most erroneous assumptions and mistakes I've seen in the academic world, and how to overcome them. I changed the workshop title to 'How to give a great presentation.' We had a full session. The postgraduates fielded many interesting questions at the end of the session. Overall, it was a good experience.

. . .

A few days later, I received a surprise email from a Mr CCH, a postgraduate student at INFORMM. The following is the email:

Dear Dr. Aisyah,
I was a participant of your talk at INFORMM two days ago. Your sharing was very interesting and beneficial. Moreover, the information you delivered is useful for my academic as well as for personal use. I attended many talks, none of them as interesting as yours which can attract me throughout the entire

3-hour talk. For this, I would like to express my gratitude towards all the kind effort you made.

I am an Evernote user (and also TED talk audience). To me, it is a revolutionary service for keeping record and entirely change the way people store information. Indeed it will bring one's personal management to the next level. I wish the service can be introduced to more people in Malaysia. Eventually it will bring positive impact to the society.

Again, thank you for the good talk. Hope to be able to join your talk in future.

Best regards,
CCH
INFORMM@USM

• • •

Lessons in academic presentations

- Where possible, say yes first. Then ask for some time to think. Don't be afraid to make mistakes as you go along.
- A mistake is a window of opportunity to be the better version of yourself.

"All the great speakers were bad speakers at first."
—Ralph Waldo Emerson

Imposter syndrome

When I was doing my Ph.D. at University of Nottingham, we needed to fulfil three things during the studies:

1. **Submit a mini report** on the 1st year, followed by a viva. On passing the viva, the conversion from MPhil. to Ph.D. would proceed.

2. **Give two 20-minute presentations** on your progress to a Wednesday seminar crowd in the 2nd year and 3rd year, respectively.

The crowd consisted of deans and professors, lecturers, all postgraduates working at the university's Centre for Biomolecular Sciences. Or literally anyone from the university who could be interested on the topics.

Attending the weekly seminars were compulsory for us. The attendance was recorded as a part of our continuing education each Ph.D. year. As a part of the crowd, I saw many postgrads gave flawlessly presentations about their research. Good confidence with fluency in communicating their work. Because they are British, my thinking goes.

One of the most memorable presentation was given by a labmate of mine. He presented his three-year work. The work was under the patent filing process. He showed 5-6 slides and talked about it; after 5 minutes ended his presentation. That was followed by gasps and a look of shock in the front audience. Where most of Professors and lecturers sat. Someone started to enquire why so short? ... My labmate confidently replied, "I presented here for the purpose of fulfilling the requirement set by the university. I could reveal so much since most of the work is actively being filed for a patent." Came the approving nods and the atmosphere returned to normal.

It was the shortest presentation ever. Presented with utmost confidence.

"Effective communication is 20% what you know and 80% how you feel about what you know."–Jim Rohn

• • •

On the contrary, nerve-wrecking is probably the closest I could describe on preparing for my 2nd year presentation. I felt not ready at all. I have this bad habit of chewing on my fingernails, nervously, as I brainstormed for ideas.

I pored over books and journal articles, looking for ideas. I remember I didn't know what to present. I felt I hardly made much progress since the first year viva. Then I compared my progress with other postgrads. I became more nervous. My brain stopped working. That I had to rev it up by 'saturating' myself with loads of coffee and milk teas. Or rather teas with milk, British-style. A cup of tea with a dash of milk.

Because the molecule has several points of modifications or features, it would look too complicated if I show everything at once.

Once revved up, I could start putting things on my Powerpoint slides. Interestingly, designing my presentation was not a linear process. If I remember correctly, I worked from the methodology section to the results, conclusion and future work. I left the introductory part to the last.

I remember I focused first on drawing the molecule of interest, that is a sugar linked benzimidazole. Because the molecule has several points of modifications or features, it would look too complicated if I show everything at once. So I decided to use the layering effect with colours, thus introducing one point at a time.

Based on a core molecule, I 'broke' the molecule into small parts. Each small part was labelled with different colours and text. These little tasks were performed in ChemDraw.

Switching to Powerpoint, I then pasted each small part into the slide and re-aligned to the core molecule. Each part got animated; they came into the slide at a cue, in a clockwise sequence. I checked this part several times to make sure the animation ran smoothly.

Because of such details and layering, this part of the work took the most time. I spent almost a week, on just one slide, in addition to the normal lab work.

Once the entire slide deck was done, I remember I practised in front of the mirror a few times, a day before my presentation. I felt confident.

• • •

The day came. I was the second presenter. Whatever the first presenter talked about went so quickly in front of me. I couldn't concentrate. My mind was more pre-occupied with my talk–what I wanted to say first followed by the next one and so on... than his.

Next came, Dub dab, Dub dab, Dub dab. It quickens as I talked. The sound of my heartbeats.

Then I heard my name being called. I went up to the computer, double clicked on my presentation and started talking. Few minutes into the talk, I could feel cold sweat. Even thought I had no recollection of the things I talked about, I could clearly remember these emotions and thoughts.

My hands were already ice-cold and shaking. My mouth was dry. Next came, Dub dab, Dub dab, Dub dab. It quickens as I talked. The sound of my heartbeats. I could hear these much louder than my own voice.

I simply couldn't turn off the chatters in my mind.

More negative thoughts came back. I remember the nervousness stayed on until half-way through. At the sight of the slide on the molecule of interest, somehow, I begin to calm down. I remember I was able to convey fluently to the audience the features of the core molecule. I could see them, especially the front ones, nodded in agreement. *Phewww…*

Unexpectedly, my nervousness flared again when it came to presenting on my synthesis workflow. The workflow consisted of a sequence of chemical reactions that I did in the last 2 years. Negative thoughts flew in, that I didn't have much progress. That the chemistry looks so simple. That it looks like an undergraduate work. What if they think my work is unworthy of the 2nd year Ph.D.? Do I sound like a chemist? What if they think I'm an imposter? Not qualified to talk about chemical synthesis.

I simply couldn't turn off the chatters in my mind. I remember I faced and talked to the slides, instead to the audience. I just committed one of the 'biggest sins' in academic presentation. *Oh dear…*

I quickly concluded my talk. The first presenter came and reassured that I gave a good presentation. To which he quickly added,

"Always believe that you know a little more than the audience."

Great advice! I remember it until this day. On confidence for any presentation.

"Twenty years from now you will be more disappointed by the things you didn't do than by the ones you did do…. Explore. Dream. Discover."
–H. Jackson Brown, Jr.

When there's no drama...

If you sit in a postgraduate research seminar, you soon would realise that an academic presentation follows a certain format. A predictable, linear vertical format; in an outline format as below:

- Title slide
- Outline of the talk
- Introduction/Background/Literature review
- Problem statement
- Aim and Objectives
- Methods
- Results and Discussions
- Conclusions
- Future Work
- References

It's very similar to a thesis format. Almost every presenter (reads, postgraduates) follows this format religiously when it comes to presenting one's work.

Only a dead person shows a flatline on the heart rate monitor.

A slight departure from this format could result in a raise eyebrow from a research supervisor or evaluation panels for research progress. It's a panacea in higher education. Or so it seems...

Interestingly, if these points are lined up horizontally, one would get a flatline. There is no drama. No heartbeats. No pulse. Only a dead person shows a flatline on the heart rate monitor. That is why an academic presentation can be so dry and dull... when one lets the left brain do all the talking and presenting.

...do you ever wonder why we can watch Bollywood films for hours?

On the other hand, do you ever wonder why we can watch Bollywood films for hours? Because it's dramatic. Because it shows the struggles and conflicts–between parents and their sons, between a boy and a girl, between a good person and an evil person. And because it is also quite relatable to our own lives. Due to these factors, we can be literally glued to the television in order to watch the ending.

One of the most impactful presentations I've been in was given by a Professor who shared her struggles in patenting her invention.

For the sake of the argument, if one draws a storyline for a typical Bollywood film, one would find that it is impossible to draw a flatline. Each turning point has almost all the ingredients that stir one's emotions—sad, happy, intriguing, joy, anger, jealousy, greed, envy and evilness. Culmination of all these emotions and the promise of a good resolution leads to the long-awaited climax. Something unmissable.

Metaphorically speaking, one can envision climbing a mountain aiming for the apex of one's career, perhaps as a Professor, as a leading authority and an expert in a particular field. In a manner of climbing a mountain, from the foothill, stepwise, your story builds on one scientific milestone at a time. Discoveries after discoveries, backtracks, U-turns, knockdowns and setbacks are the milestones, rewards and struggles to get to the top.

One of the most impactful presentations I've been in was given by a Professor who shared her struggles in patenting her invention. As the university threatened to take her to the court for fraud, she did some detective work to find the culprit. She took upon herself to scrutinise all laboratory results related to the patent.

The turning point came when she found that the results had been 'professionally' doctored to mislead her and other people. The culprit was identified; it's her 'good' student who submitted 'perfect' results for the patent filing. Eventually, the Professor had her name cleared from the accusations and defamation.

That the struggles are real. They make us human... Such stories should be shared.

The majority of academicians prefer to narrate a story of achievements. Many refuse to open their cupboards full of skeletons of failures and struggles. Understandably, perhaps due to the fear of humiliation, feeling vulnerable or the ego gets in the way. The above story, not only left a lasting impact, but also I learned a lesson (or two) about the scientific enterprise.

That the struggles are real. They make us human. Contained therein are character-building stories, lessons and wisdoms. Such stories should be shared.

Can you imagine presenting your academic work in this manner?

Lessons in academic presentations

- **A hero's journey.** A good story transports listeners into the presenter's world. Struggles, conflicts followed by resolutions are elements of a good story.
- **Putting oneself in the presenter's shoes.** When these elements are included in an academic presentation, they unlock the presenter's world to listeners, through emotions and empathy. A listener, thereby, can empathise with the presenter's situations and challenges.
- **Share struggles in your academic presentations.** To turn a dull, dry academic presentation to a great one, don't hesitate to inject a bit of drama, lessons and wisdoms from your own research pain points and struggles in your next presentation.

"Stories are our primary tools of learning and teaching, the repositories of our lore and legends. They bring order into our confusing world. Think about how many times a day you use stories to pass along data, insights, memories, or common-sense advice."–Edward Miller

How NOT to look boring

An academic presentation is so predictable. It uses a familiar-looking Powerpoint template, is crammed with text and has little or no images. Looks like a document. And reads like a document...

To look boring is easy. It's almost everywhere in higher education settings. So now... how to turn an academic presentation into an interesting visual treat remains a challenge for both academics and students. Here I share some simple tips to turn any academic Powerpoint presentations from boring to looking great!

Type (Font)

Use sans serif, instead of serif. For example, change from Times New Roman to Arial or Calibri. Typically, Times New Roman works well for documents or articles where people spend time reading long text.

A presentation is briefer. I recommend one idea per slide. And don't forget about the size. The bigger the room you'll be presenting, the bigger the text should be. My rule of thumb for font size in a 150-capacity lecture hall is anywhere between 28-36, minimum.

So it is a good idea to check the venue, a day before you presentation. Get the feel of the room.

Don't cram everything…

on 1-3 slides. I understand you spend 6-9 months, say on reviewing 100's of articles and books during the literature review phase. But that doesn't mean overloading the slides (and your presentation) with a massive amount of information. Spread out the main points in 4-5 slides.

An indispensable skill, but often overlooked, is the skill in presenting the essence and its relevance to your thesis.

During the literature review stage, if unsure, ask yourself, "what are 3 key contributions of this article?" and "how would these key contributions relate to my study?" Then, share 1 main point with the panel/audience. Learning how to distil the essence of an area or a body of knowledge is a skill essential to any researcher.

An indispensable skill, but often overlooked, is the skill in presenting the essence and its relevance to your thesis. I believe, one should continue cultivating for brevity and clarity in communicating and presenting your ideas and work in the academic setting.

Avoid cramming. Avoid verbosity. The adverse effects of more text in a presentation are boredom and sleep. A 'cure' for insomnia…

References

Highlight the top 3 articles. Make them visual–screen capture the titles and authors of the articles. The slide with the rest of 10+ articles can be placed after the 'Thank you' slide, in case any evaluators or academics are interested to find out further.

Of course, there are more elements in a presentation that one can manipulate to elevate your presentations. The elements and choices in a presentation range from the wise use of spaces, colours, images and layouts. Choose an appropriate presentation delivery using a storyline. The elements are always under the surface. Invisible to the unaware.

"That's not what we think design is. It's not just what it looks like and feels like. Design is how it works."
–Steve Jobs

• • •

Lessons in academic presentations

- Learn to distill the essence of the important work in your field. Summarise 3 key contributions per paper.
- Avoid cramming everything in a slide. Keep an academic presentation light and simple.

- For fonts size in a 150-capacity lecture hall is anywhere between 28-36, minimum. For a huge room, e.g. a ballroom, use bigger fonts.
- Being super aware of design elements and choices in a presentation goes beyond cosmetics. A well-designed presentation helps you communicate your ideas in a clear and convincing manner to move and transform an audience beyond their own expectations.
That's a successful presentation!

For any academic presentations, keep it light and simple...

Learn from Jack Ma

I was invited as a panel for a 3-minute thesis (3MT) at a faculty. It's an all women panel. It's the first time the faculty organised such event. The presenters were Ph.D. students at the faculty. Originated in University of Queensland, Australia, the 3MT competition is an awesome way for a postgraduate students to learn how to package a 3-year Ph.D. work into 180 seconds. Super concise presentation that makes sense to educated people.

I noticed that most new presenters made the same mistake. They tend to fix themselves in one spot. As if their feet were anchored to the very spot, thus unable to move. They hardly work the room. They looked timid, nervous and shy as they presented.

Watch Jack Ma delivering his talk. Jack Ma walks from one end of the stage to the next. He times his steps to emphasise certain points. His body language (non-verbal) is in synchrony with his speech. He owns the space.

Lessons in academic presentations

- By working the room, you are telling people non-verbally that you own the space.
- Always keep learning from the best.

5. Thoughts on Preparation, Design and Delivery in Academic Presentations

Planning

Ideas-storming

Malaysia being a tropical country, we are never far from occasional thunderstorms during the rainy season. Where huge dark 'cauliflower' clusters of cumulonimbus clouds steadily march on and discharge heavy rains, along with flashes of lightning and deep, rumbling thunders.

'Brainstorming' could have sounded as scary as thunderstorms, but you know it is not. Brainstorming is an essential part, if not the first part, in planning your next presentation. Though I prefer the word ideation rather than brainstorming.

...the yellow sticky notes, by far, is the most effective tools for planning my presentations.

I receive ideas, stories for my presentations while surfing the net, driving, having coffee, chatting with friends and in the shower. The latter is perhaps when the most ideas come. It is the most vulnerable yet comfortable situation one could be–ideas simply rushing in, without much coaxing. In many instances, the ideas refuse to budge; they keep coming and knocking on my door... until I find it a place to keep them.

Sticky notes are where I keep my ideas. You may find index cards, mind mapping or quick writing on a whiteboard useful; the yellow sticky notes, by far, is the most effective tools for planning my presentations. It makes the planning session productive. Each mimics a slide. I jot down 1-2 idea on each sticky note, as the ideas come. The next thing I do is to arrange them in a sequence as to how I want to deliver my presentation. This is designing the flow–structuring of the story for a presentation.

"The best way to get a good idea is to have a lot of ideas."
–Linus Pauling

I learned so many useful tips from my workshop participants. At a lunch, a Professor revealed her presentation secrets, "In the beginning of my research, I normally asked my students to do Powerpoint for the conferences that I would present. About a month before the conferences, I asked them to do presentations. I checked the slides, I told them revise a few things here and there. However, with experience, interestingly the story appears in my mind a day or two before my keynote or plenary." The Professor added with a playful smile, "... it's not something you can force though."

Essential in any brainstorming session is to never cross out any idea. Every idea is accepted.

As you gain more experience in a field, it gets easier to find a story structure or 'storyline' for your teaching and research presentations. For postgraduates and young academics, it is a vital stage that can't be overlooked.

Essential in any brainstorming session is to never cross out any idea. Every idea is accepted. Something you can do it on your own or in groups. The next part, after brainstorming, is finding clarity.

Lessons in academic presentations

- Find a place to keep your most precious ideas. It could be an app (I use iA Writer or Notes), a Word document, a notepad, a Moleskin or even at the back of a napkin. Keep them well and in a place where you can easily find them. You certainly thank me for the suggestion (you're welcome), but you will thank yourself for doing so because you will never know when 'the stars are aligned'.

- In groups, having each idea is accepted at this stage will set the tone and dynamics of the group. Each person matters, that is the message you want to convey and established early as a leader.
- Sticky pads, notebooks, mind mapping, a wall or whiteboard—find a workable, fun way to place, arrange and re-arrange your ideas.
- Find a flexible and creative way to mapping your ideas, work and present them as a story.
- Structuring a story, or story boarding, in a presentation is essential. A global view of your presentation, a story board can serve as the foundation for future work.

A global view of your presentation, a story board can serve as the foundation for future work.

Planning

Finding Clarity

In the previous lesson, ideally you have a lot of ideas in the brainstorming part. Perhaps you dig deep and found your why. Perhaps you have a rough structure of your story. It may cross your mind, how will clarity help me in preparing my presentation?

Many presenters start their presentations by opening a MS Powerpoint and start outlining their ideas and hammering those words. Words after words, after wooords. Or oohhh let's copy paste some text from my earlier articles or some office documents.

Because data dumping is not a presentation.

Then add in some visuals, an icon here, 1-2 images there. Keep doing that until... right we have put in all the information needed here. Fantastic, lots of things already in there. Now let's just put in a conclusion and future work slide. Okay, that would do it. It should engage my audience (Inner thoughts: I'm happy with my slides). On the presentation day, it turns out worse than you had expected. Because data dumping is not a presentation.

An audience can sniff this disaster from afar.

Another instance is when you find your audience seems tuned in. As you speak, you can see nods, smiles and all eyes on you. They participate in all your interactive activities throughout the session. Good, positive body language. You are happy to see that they seem engaged in the session. But how do you really know? Some might be feigning interests...

Faking interest: Telltale signs
A telltale sign is when your audience ask you a basic question on something you thought you had already elaborated in your presentation.

- As the session at an infographic workshop for students was coming to a close, a student suddenly raised her hand and asked, "Doctor, what is an infographic?"
- At a design thinking workshop, during the Q&A session (after a 1-hour hands-on session), a participant was overheard asking the trainer, "If you don't mind me asking as I am not clear, What is design thinking?"

So what went wrong? Lack of clarity in meaning and purpose could spell a disaster for a presenter. An audience can sniff this disaster from afar. That the first impression matters. The thing about an audience: *they are quite forgiving*. They would go along with you, as to not cause you any embarrassment in public. Asking 1-2 quick questions along the way to test their understanding or that they are following you is important in any presentation. I learned this the hard way.

The secret in captivating presentations
Here I am sharing with you a secret of a presentation. Besides story, your clarity of purpose is your secret weapon in captivating your audience. Your clarity help to extinguish all anxiety and nervousness when delivering your presentation. Your clarity helps you present in a more authentic manner.

Besides story, your clarity of purpose is your secret weapon in captivating your audience.

Writing your big ideas down to target a defined audience will make your purpose pop up, the big idea becomes crystal clear–to you. Next tie those points with your audience's needs–What is in for me? (WIIFM). To find out, it is a habit of mine to pose the question in the beginning of a workshop. "What do you want to gain by the end of this session?" Empty your minds and listen deeply to their WIIFMs.

Use these big ideas to navigate your audience in your talk.

Match and blend your big ideas with your audience's WIIFMs. Paraphrase them and introduce the big ideas intentionally at strategic places in your presentation. Use these big ideas to navigate your audience in your talk. Navigate your audience to what they would gain from listening to you. That would be the benefits, with the big B.

An exercise in finding clarity

In the comment box below, note down 3 messages that you want your audience to take home. Something memorable and unforgettable for your audience. If it helps, visualise your target audience.

Imagine they go home with your take-home messages. Imagine how excited they would be of something new they learn from your talk. Imagine how they'd continue talking about your seminar for days later.

Simply because you have clearly driven home your messages which deeply resonate with your audience. You have helped them see the light at the end of the tunnel. You may have helped them solve their problems.

As an exercise, take time to write 3 take-home messages for your audience:

1. By the end of my talk, I want _____.

2. By the end of my talk, I want _____.

3. By the end of my talk, my audience must know why I share _____.

Lessons in academic presentations

- Don't leave home without your 3 take-home messages.
- Communicate your 3 take-home messages (or benefits) at the start of your presentation.
- Find out your audience's WIIFM.
- Tie the WIIFM and your take home messages together. This will make your presentation more memorable and impactful for your audience.

Planning and Design

Invite Creative Energy

If you observe kids painting, there's so much freedom in their expressions. A kid's mind is tabula rasa. No content. Just a blank slate.

A blank space invites creative energy to enter. A blank space lets relevant (and irrelevant) things to come in and go. The 'things' feel free to re-arrange themselves and slowly settle until before the presentation day. That's why I always start with a blank slide.

A blank space invites creative energy to enter.

It is very gratifying to start a presentation from a blank slide and building it up as I go along. A layer at a time. An idea per slide. I could adjust the colours and layouts accordingly. Few more reasons I rarely use a template.

That said, I'm aware many of Powerpoint or Keynote users find templates useful. Templates help increase productivity. Templates take care of slide designs. And at times, let the mind rests. Templates allow users to focus more on the content or subject matter.

To this end, the latest Microsoft Powerpoint features Powerpoint Designer. The feature uses artificial intelligence that suggest a number of designs based on the content of your slides. Sway in Microsoft 365 does something similar.

I understand you have KPIs to chase, papers to write, students presentations, full day meetings to attend. Adopting a beginner's mind to invite creative energy that could bring originality and inventiveness into your work. Yet, keep an eye open for possibilities and technology that help enhancing your productivity at work.

"In the beginner's mind there are many possibilities, but in the expert's there are few."
–Shunryu Suzuki.

Design

Learn to say No

A well-designed presentation relies in our ability to say No.
- "Shall I copy and paste text from my paper, then dump them into the slides?" No.
- Where do you want to place these photos? "What about putting these photos anywhere near the text?" Anywhere? No.
- "Make those photos small ya... They are just to decorate the slides. The text is more important." No.
- "Can you squeeze one more point into the slide?" The slide already looks quite full. No.

Fundamentally, each slide is an empty canvas. It needs an underlying structure, a layout, that is usually invisible to non-designers. Skills in visual literacy can be learned.

...colours can be used to highlight, unify and invoke emotions.

As described earlier, we can learn about hierarchy from a Japanese Garden. Hierarchy informs the audience the priority and importance of the information on a slide. The spaces between 2 elements indicate relationship; closer could mean they are related, far away means otherwise. If two related elements are placed far apart, it would confuse to the audience—is the presenter saying the two elements related or not? Besides these, we can use colours to highlight, unify and invoke emotions.

Using simple design principles and choices, an academic presenter will be able to bring out the beauty of his or her message. Design elevates a presenter's message above the noise. It lets the message sounds like a beautiful music to your audience's ears.

"The music is not in the notes, but in the silence between."–Mozart

Design and Delivery

ACE That Presentation!

How do you prepare days or a week before your big presentation day? What do you do?...

Preparing to deliver your presentation starts from the core. The core is your authentic self and your message to the world. The 'A' in ACE stands for authenticity, where your true power resides. Next are C and E. The 'C' stands for compelling and 'E' for engaging.

To deliver a compelling and engaging presentation, I believe one has to craft a story with your core message embedded. Combining these with powerful visuals and data to illustrate and support your story and points are a surefire way to engage your audience–thus, 'ACEing' both their hearts and minds.

To deliver a compelling and engaging presentation, I believe one has to craft a story with your core message embedded.

In addition to these general model, I've noted down below the thoughts and questions I find useful in my own process:

A week before

First, check the program details. Where is the venue? When is your presentation? Are you the first presenter? Often the first speaker sets the tone for the rest of the session. Or will you be presenting in-between 2-3 speakers? If you are, do check out the titles of the speakers before and after.

The answers to these questions could serve the invisible structures of your story.

The information will give you some ideas of the tone and theme of the session. You could pick up some ideas or points you find relevant to your presentation. Gauge the impact of your talk to the speakers and audience.

Then, visualise the conference venue and think about:
- How the room would look like?
- How would the audience be like?
- How would you want to take them on a journey?
- How would you open the presentation?
- How you would want them respond to your points?

- How many points will you be making, what are they?

Apart from these questions, imagine how would you want to end the talk? With a quote, a story or a video of the future to sum up your conclusions?

The answers to these questions could serve the invisible structures of your story, a storyline of your presentation. Every presentation has to have, at least, a story or otherwise, it would turn out quite dry.

Why practice? Practice helps you become familiar with the content, iron out inconsistencies and builds iron-clad confidence on the stage.

Write out the speech

With these notes written down, it'll be easier to start putting the flesh to the storyline. Write out the text for your presentation. If it is convenient, start in the point form.

As I go through each slide, I would note down 3 points. Powerpoint includes a productivity tool in drafting the script–turn on the presenter's view at the bottom of each Powerpoint slide. Other useful apps are a text editor (e.g. iA Writer, MS Word) or if you prefer to go online, there's Evernote or OneNote. This is your first draft script.

Practice runs

At the end of writing the speech, do a practice run. I use Evernote because it combines a text editor with a recorder. After writing down my speech, I straightaway record my speech as I read it out loud. This read-out-loud practice tremendously helps me in tweaking the speech. As I go along, I would edit words/sentences, the tone and pace of my delivery. Why practice? Practice helps you become familiar with the content, irons out inconsistencies and builds iron-clad confidence on the stage.

> *...if you are given 20 minutes, aim to finish in 18 minutes.*

Additionally, I take note of the duration of reading the speech. It should be about 80-90% of the allocated time. For example, if you are given 20 minutes, aim to finish in 18 minutes. It's considered 'presentation bad manners' to go over the allocated time. Additionally, it will eat into the next speakers' time. The remaining 2 minutes is ample for any technical error or a room to improve or elaborate a point, should you feel a need.

Alternatively, you may want to video record yourself as if you're giving a presentation. No DSLR camera, no worries. You can do screencast/video selfie using your mobile devices, laptop or PC. Just read the text, it's OK on practice runs. With more rehearsals, you'd gain familiarity and confidence over your presentation.

A few days before the big day

Practice without the 'training wheels'. Run through your draft slide deck without reading from the speech.
- Be mindful of the tone and pace of your delivery.
- Be aware of your body language as you practice. Which slide(s) that I tend to forget my points and go um..?
- Anchor your speech to the slide(s) by inserting key points or better an image with 1-2 key point(s).
- Practise in front of an audience. Find trusted colleagues or friends of yours. Ask for honest and specific feedback on your rehearsal.

When you're invited to the podium, greet the audience with a smile.

The big day

If you need to travel, if possible, arrange to arrive a day before. Travelling can be a hassle especially if delayed. This arrangement helps you to calm your nerves and re-frames your mind to the task at hand.

When you reach the venue, possibly 1-2 hours ahead, find the technical guys first. Discuss your technical needs, particularly if you have specialised needs for example using a Mac (needs an adapter) or wish to present using iPad or

Prezi (needs to be downloaded and/or with an internet connection).

Some conferences prefer to collect Powerpoint from all presenters prior to the presentation session. Get ready with a Powerpoint or a pdf. Don't forget to include a CC licence on the title slide, if you plan to share your presentation.

When you're invited to the podium, greet the audience with a smile and launch your well-rehearsed presentation. It's time for you to shine and ACE That Presentation!

Good luck!

"Some entrepreneurs think how can I make a lot of money? But a better way is to think how can I make people's lives a lot better? If you get it right, the money will come." – Richard Branson

Delivery

Doctor, can you do a Powerpoint workshop?

―――――――

Everything that has a beginning... My workshop 'Presentation Makeover for Educators' began from a request for a Powerpoint workshop for School Secretaries. It was a request from Puan Hajar Zituakmar Mohd Fauzi, then an Assistant Registrar at School of Pharmaceutical Sciences.

Initially, I was quite surprised to get such request. Why would secretaries for Deans and Deputy Deans need a workshop on Powerpoint? Often, it's a lecturer in a School or Institute who would design slides for a Dean/Director's presentation. Puan Hajar explained that the secretaries needed to sit for exams on certain Microsoft apps– Powerpoint is one of them.

Err... I'm not a Powerpoint user, I told Puan Hajar but I can help you. So I studied the basic features of Powerpoint and combined them with many simple examples that explain the four principles in visual design. Took about 1.5 months to come up with the entire workshop materials. But I was happy of how things turned out. The workshop went well. It received comments from the workshop participants, some are as follows:

"Well-planned and very informative workshop that I've ever attended for IT workshop in USM. Good job to Dr. Aisyah!"

"Can invite lecturers to join this workshop."

"Kursus yang sangat berguna kepada semua setiausaha yang menyediakan 'powerpoint presentation' kepada bos masing-masing. Diajar oleh Dr. Aisyah Saad yang sangat mahir di dalam bidang tersebut walaupun berbeza bidang di PPSF (Pusat Pengajian Sains Farmasi)." (Translation: A course that is very useful to all secretaries in preparing powerpoint presentations for their respective bosses. Taught by Dr. Aisyah Saad whom is very skilful in the field even though the field differs from those fields in PPSF, the School of Pharmacy)

"I feel comfortable and easily adapted with the friendly environment, especially by the presenter."

"All session is very good and the workshop give a good deal of information about Powerpoint."

• • •

> *There is a time and place for everything, I consoled myself and kept the dream alive.*

I remember years earlier, when my teaching slides were featured in the classic presentation book, Presentation Zen by Garr Reynolds, I approached some key people at the university's training department (HR).

I wanted to offer workshops for educators and staff, but it was declined. The top officer took a look at my slides in the book and said, "(slides) like these... you can ask your son or daughter to do it. I don't see the need to offer training on Powerpoint."

There is a time and place for everything, I consoled myself and kept the dream alive.

• • •

In 2014, thanks to Prof. Abd Karim Alias, CDAE@USM Director, provided me the space and ample opportunities in offering such workshops to fellow educators and researchers. Presentation Makeover for Educators grew from there on.

The workshop was offered twice a year. The materials from the Powerpoint workshop for secretaries were further fine-tuned to suit educators. The first workshop was called 'Designing Effective Presentation'. After a series of these workshops, I felt 'Presentation Makeover for Educators' is a more suitable name. Even though the workshop title seems focused towards educators; the workshop has been attended by senior and junior lecturers (Professors included), librarians, postdoctoral researchers and scientists.

They decided to stay on because they found the workshop was more interesting than the (concurrent Professorial) talk.

I remember one workshop I conducted at the university's health campus in the east coast of Malaysia. At the beginning of the workshop, it was already about 20 educators from various departments and schools–dental, nursing, medicine and health sciences. Thirty minutes into the session, one by one walked in. Suddenly I was told that the room was already packed, there was no more computer available. It came close to 40 participants!

During the morning break, I asked the new participants why they came in late. Apparently, there was a concurrent Professorial Talk, but they left the talk to find out about my workshop. They decided to stay on because they found the workshop was more interesting than the talk. I was surprised and thanked them for coming.

That's a strong motivation to continue offering the workshop for those working and studying in the higher education settings.

When old slides get a makeover, the way they present will also change.

Many presentations suffer from poor design choices in communicating your message. In the Presentation Makeover workshop, participants learn simple design principles to turn their presentation slides from dull to beautiful. Knowledge in simple design principles for text, photos, diagrams and colours allow you to communicate your intended message with clarity.

My role is to awaken them on ways that elevate their presentations.

Not only that, participants will benefit from many presentation secrets, strategies and delivery tips that I use in my keynote talk and workshops. Unlike any other presentation workshops, participants in this workshop would re-design their old slides. When old slides get a makeover, the way they present would also change. The workshop participants would also receive feedback from fellow participants and yours truly.

At the end of the workshop, the participants would become more aware of the elements essential to bring about clarity and beauty to a presentation. My role is to awaken them on ways that elevate their presentations.

Lessons in academic presentations

- We are creative. But our education systems taught us to believe otherwise.
- There is time and place for everything.
- Never give up. Never give up. *Never* give up.

"When you learn to trust yourself implicitly, you no longer need to prove something through your art. You simply allow it to come out, to be as it is. This is when creating art becomes effortless. It happens just as you grow your hair. It grows."
–John Daido Loori in The Zen of Creativity.

6. Proceed, if you dare…

Apples or Oranges

Once upon a time, there were hot debates on which computer a better computer? Whether it's Apple Macintosh or PCs? Leveraging on this debate, Apple made a series of clever short video commercials that went viral. The videos showed amusing banters between a good looking next door guy in casual clothing and a nerdy bespectacled office worker. The videos started with:

> Mac: Hello I'm a Mac
> PC: And I'm a PC
> And we have a lot in common these days,
> except when... (suddenly PC hangs... Moments later)
> PC: Sorry, I had to restart.
> (The reason why I switched to a Mac)

What if the same question is asked for presentations, which computer is better at creating beautiful presentations? Here is a story about two fictitious academics, Dr. X and Dr. Y.

When Dr. X bought his first MacBook, he did all his teaching presentations using Apple Keynote. Students were impressed, they said Dr. X lectures were special, gave beautiful presentations. So the word-of-mouth spread.

The word reached Dr. Y, who had lots of grant money. Because Dr. Y wanted so much to create beautiful presentations like Dr. X, every time Apple announced the release of new Mac laptops and desktop, Dr. Y would be the first one on campus to buy them.

Dr. Y would find an opportunity to show off new 'Apple conquests' to Dr. X. On one occasion, Dr. Y even bought the largest Apple Macintosh–the Super-sized Big Mac. It's the first thing Dr. X saw when he entered Dr. Y's office. Emerging from behind the enormous screen, Dr. Y greeted Dr. X, "Hey X, look at my new iMac. What do you think?"

Dr. X smiled and said, "Wow, you have outdone yourself. The huge screen is great for work and pictures, and of course, presentations." The good doctor grinned from ear to ear. Only later, Dr. X realised the unwanted effect; that Dr. Y was actually fishing for Dr. X's compliment to boost his ego.

Months had passed before Dr. X and Dr. Y met again at a students' progress meeting. After several rounds of presentations, a student of Dr. Y presented the research progress. That drew a praise from Dr. X, who went on saying to the student, "Wow! That was a good presentation. And I was amazed at the beautiful animal models. Did you draw that? How did you do it?"

The student replied yes, and went on explaining in great detail how he searched for the right animal models and carefully modified the colours, background, shadows to achieve the beautiful look. It took him a few weeks to do the detailing on the models.

Looking puzzled, Dr. Y asked the student, "Did you use a Mac to do all that??"

"No, I used the PCs in our lab," the student replied.

Dr. Y looked even more surprised, and blurted out, "So you don't need an Apple Macintosh to do beautiful slides. Any PC can do the same or better??!..." *Double facepalm*

Since then, Dr. Y was seen going around on campus with a slim Windows-based laptop. Apparently, this incident had left a big impact on Dr. Y. It changed his perception on the best computer for creating a beautiful presentation.

Lessons in academic presentations

- Apples or Oranges? You decide. A good presentation doesn't have to rely on expensive tools. One can still create stunning presentation using one's ingenuity and creativity.
- We must learn and know how to use a tool well to create and offer a solution for a common good. That's what matters, above all.

One can still create stunning presentation using one's ingenuity and creativity.

I am Nothing

In a communication skills workshop for educators, the trainer went around asking each participant to share 'Who are you?" The idea is that you should know yourself enough to be able to communicate to your audience. So the microphone went around, the session got busy with genuine, quirky answers from the participants. Some answers:

"I am a father, an educator."

"I am a researcher."

"I am a determined person."

"I am Me."

"I am Nothing," came my reply.

That surprised many people including the trainer. The trainer tried to tone it down by saying, "Why nothing...-you are somebody?"

I smiled at her attempts to reassure me. My colleague nearby gently asked, "Why did you say that?"

"If you strip away everything–material possessions, children, friends, titles, ego–what are you left with? Your body and your Self. Your spirit. Just like when we are born into the world this way, we will leave the world this way too," came my reply. She went quiet. When you let go and accept things as they are, it feels lighter and much easier to rise higher.

Life cycle of lecture slides

My colleagues and friends have been asking me, "Why you spent so much energy and time on presentations and students activities? Why can't you be more like other academics?"

"What do you mean?" I asked my colleagues. "Simply copy and paste text and diagrams into Powerpoint, then read from my slides?"

They replied, "Yes, anyway you will share that Powerpoint slides with your students. They will use the slides for their notes and revisions. So why bother?..."

The life cycle of lecture slides: At the end of the year, keep the lecture slides in your hard drive or Google Drive. One hour before the lecture, revise what to teach. Talk for 50 minutes. If forgotten, read from text-laden slides. Share it with students. Rinse and repeat in the next academic session. The most efficient way of teaching?

Many lecturers seem to think and do so. Where dated lecture slides (from 1990s) are still in circulation. Where the learning management system (LMS) is still being treated like a glorified Dropbox. Where effort in improving teaching and learning tend to go unnoticed.

I'm happy to see and hear the practice is changing with the implementation of blended learning. Yet, I am most troubled when teaching remains stagnant, simply recycled.

Stollen recipe

This is a fictitious story about a blue stollen recipe. The takeaways from this story could apply to academics.

In a galaxy far, far away from the Milky Way, there is a prosperous kingdom of blue-coloured intelligent and hardworking little men and women. They are known as the Smaarphs. In the Smaarph kingdom, one of the most-prized breads is a blue stollen. It is the most delicious, softest and aromatic bread that has the lightest hue of blue. A bite of the blue stollen also chases the blues away for the entire day. In other words, the blue stollen is an effective antidepressant in the Smaarph kingdom.

Though any Smaarph can bake a stollen, no one could imitate the delicious blue stollen.

In the kingdom, only two Smaarphs, A and B, know how to make the stollen. The bakery owner B inherits the blue stollen recipe from his family, whereas A is a baker apprentice to B. She's a hard worker who starts early morning to open the bakery and works late every day. Eventually A gains the trust of B. Baker B teaches A the recipe of the blue stollen. In time, A bakes beautiful stollens for Smaarph B bakery. B asks his apprentice not to reveal the recipe of the blue stollen.

The word of mouth goes around Smaarph kingdom that A has the blue stollen recipe but has sworn to secrecy.

Many attempted to bribe A to reveal the recipe but unsuccessful.

The story reaches Smaarph C, another bakery owner, who wants to seize the opportunity just for himself. Coming from a big poor family, he always dreams a life of prestige, privileges and power. That if he could steal the blue stollen recipe from B, he would be the richest man in the entire Galaxy. So C uses all the tricks to persuade A to join his bakery. Promises after promises are poured to A. It seems that A is not easily persuaded.

Then C conceives another devilish plot. C cooks untrue stories about his son's faithful wife leading him to divorce his wife. Smaarph C devises ways so that his heartbroken son D falls in love with A.

True to C plans, A and D fall in love and subsequently marry. A joins the bakery of Smaarph C. Not long after, the highly prized blue stollens start to appear on the shelves of C bakery. But C wants more; he is not happy simply baking for the kingdom.

Smaarph C wants to go big and loves the limelight. Opportunist in nature, C patents the blue stollen recipe, naming himself, A and his son D as the inventors. Smaarph C scales up the production of blue stollens by building factories and export the breads to other kingdoms in the Galaxy. Soon, demands exceed supply. Smaarph C is over the moon.

When the words get to B, he confronts C. But C doesn't want to back out, continues to exert his ownership of the blue stollen recipe. Unhappy, B requests an audience with the Smaarph King about the stollen recipe. The King grants the request and sees B. The invitation for an audience with the King is extended to C but he doesn't come. During the meet, the King is informed that the exported blue stollens from C has brought about fame for the kingdom. To B's surprise, the King advisers accuse B trying to damage the reputation and prestige of the Smaarph Kingdom.

In his defence, B says that the blue stollen recipe has been in his family for generations. That, these Smaarphs are not the inventors; in fact, they steal the blue stollen recipe without his knowledge, then they claim they invented the recipe but actually they are the thieves. The King waves his hand dismissing B's defence and abruptly ends the meet.

Later, B learns from his informants that C has had an audience with the King and his advisers earlier, and promises a weekly lifetime supply of blue stollens to the palace. For free.

During the King's birthday the following year, Smaarphs A, C and D receive OBE awards for their outstanding contributions to the kingdom of Smaarphs.

These events shatter the worldview of B. He turns his journey inwards towards healing; it took years before he begins to trust anyone in the Smaarph kingdom. The reality of living in the Smaarph kingdom teaches him life's greatest lessons:

- Intellectual property thieves wouldn't think twice about stealing one's hard work. They want all the

glory, and bask in the limelight, even when the work is not theirs.
- Intellectual thieves hide behind many masks. It takes time to identify them. Possible telltale signs are victim tales, the love of limelight and power hungry.
- A sure sign is shamelessness and/or guilt-free when confronted with their unprofessional behaviours. They get angry and threatened you if they're exposed. So take care of yourself first.
- Unscrupulous people, like A and C, are skilled at manipulating a system and people. Under manipulations, the system serves to protect and support such people. Where greed begets more greed, and thieves prosper.

A presentation on your research results, for example, if it falls into the wrong hands, may give rise to papers, book chapters and KPIs for the academic rogue. To save yourselves from such academic horror stories, make sure you protect your intellectual property by copyright or licensing it under Creative Commons.

It could well be your colleagues working under the same roof or institution.

Everyone has a story worth telling

Everyone has a story written for them, in their hearts they know. Rather, they knew. If the purpose of life is to find meaning, maybe that's a part of what Life is. But perhaps the purpose of life is to play out the the story that has been written for you—by The All Mighty, The All Wise. With lessons to be learned by the character—getting scratched, hurt, bruised, broken, healed, rejuvenate. Character building, all in all.

Have you ever wondered *why* is that there is a certain longing for a certain things in a person, by not in another? Could that be the story needs to be told, needs to be expressed? The aching. The irresistible pull. All in the heart. Your story has been written, you are born to live that story, to act it out.

When it's meant for you, the universe conspires for you to achieve it.

One day I went for lunch with a friend of my late dad. She told me that when she came home with a Masters degree she applied for a lectureship position in Penang. She was interviewed for the position. She received an offer but, for some reasons, decided to decline. Close to forty years later, fate brings her back to Penang. She holds the top position at one of the leading private universities. *When it's meant for you, the universe conspires for you to achieve it.*

Why would you play less or play a lesser role in unfolding your own story? God has given and endowed you the heart, mind and all senses to lead the story of this Life, of your life. He has afforded you *time* and *resources*. Why would you go live another person's story?

• • •

This text was written on an Emirates flight to Amman, Jordan. It was a journey that I've dreamed about since I was in Cardiff as an undergraduate. I chanced upon a photo of 'Susan Sontag, Petra, Jordan' by Annie Leibovitz. It's a photo of Susan Sontag standing in the narrow pass, dramatically appearing so tiny, as compared to the ancient Al-Khazneh temple. A photo that burns in my mind ever since.

Twenty years had passed before I realised my dream journey. Jordan is magical, to say the least. In Amman, I found the book, **The Forty Rules of Love: A Novel of Rumi**, *a mystical love story between Ella and Aziz, in* parallel with Rumi and Shams of Tabriz. It's story of how the loss of his beloved leads to the radical transformation of Rumi, from a scholar to a poet.

The journey has also led to my first ebook, **Solo Jordan**, a pictorial travel guide for independent solo female travellers. A book to inspire the inner travel bugs.

"A good traveler has no fixed plans and is not intent on arriving.
A good artist lets his intuition leads him to wherever it wants.
A good scientist has freed himself of concepts and keeps his mind open to what is."
–Lao Tzu
(Tao Te Ching, chapter 27, translation by Stephen Mitchell)

7. Confessions of an introverted educator

What goes behind the screen?

My venture into do-it-yourself (DIY) video production began almost 3 years ago. It began by identifying and overcoming my fears and insecurities. My introvertedness. Voice, face, speech and screencasting tools to name a few considerations for DIY video production. Acquiring additional skills is a journey on its own–comparable to learning to give live lectures.

Giving a live lecture wasn't that difficult in the beginning of my career as a lecturer. I remember my first lecture. I walked into DK X lecture hall with my thermos and a white MacBook. Came in well-prepared, days earlier. Set it up and started talking to students. Yes, I was nervous. I talked fast.

It's a persona. On-the-stage personality in front of 120 pharmacy students.

I read from the slides. I talked and walked across the big lecture hall, pacing myself to shake off my nervousness. The excess energy. I had to act and be seen as confident and knowledgeable. No one was allowed to speak (Oh dear...).

Looking back, I realised it must have been really passive and oppressive for students. Perhaps seemed arrogant or stand-offish to some people. It's a persona. On-the-stage personality in front of 120 pharmacy students. I didn't really like it, neither enjoyed doing so.

It's for the job, but it's not me.

Through experiences conducting lectures and workshops, I came to understand myself better. I prefer working with a small group (4-5 people) than a big crowd of 120 students. One to one is the best. Often, after an hour lecturing to my students, I would lock myself in my office, lights off. I prefer living in a small city like Penang or Munich (a small big city, I call it) than metropolis in the likes of Kuala Lumpur, New York or London.

Giving myself permission to recharge by being on my own is essential for my wellbeing. That's an Aha moment—thanks to the book Quiet.

You would find me in cafes, bookshops and libraries than huge malls e.g. Pavilion KL. Spending more than a couple of hours in big cities or with crowds would irritate and exhaust me. Giving myself permission to recharge by being on my own is essential for my wellbeing. That's an Aha moment–thanks to the book Quiet: The Power of Introverts in a World That Can't Stop Talking.

So I'm an introverted lecturer. But how to thrive in the academic world where meeting, dining and collaborating with people seem to be more rewarding than working quietly on my own?

I've learned how to speak from my heart and be present with my audience.

Over the years, I acquire a few more tricks up my sleeves to calm the nerves down and conserve my energy for a long workshop. I learn to conquer my nervousness by looking at friendly faces in the sea of students and doing deep breathing in/out just before saying the first word.

Even after umpteenth number of lectures and workshops, nervousness likes to pay a visit. Just before a big talk. Though it's much gentler now on my nerves because I welcome and embrace it, rather than fending it off. I've learned how to speak from my heart and be present with my audience. That's with live lectures and workshops.

So, what goes behind the screen?

Accepting My Voice

I thought if I could talk non-stop for 1 hour to my students, of course I could just wing it for video recording. Just press record, talk, talk, talk and if needed, press pause. After 1 hour, press stop and upload to youtube. Additionally, recording videos than giving lectures would probably work in favour of my introverted nature. I convinced myself it'd be much easier than giving live lectures.

Nothing could be further from the truth.

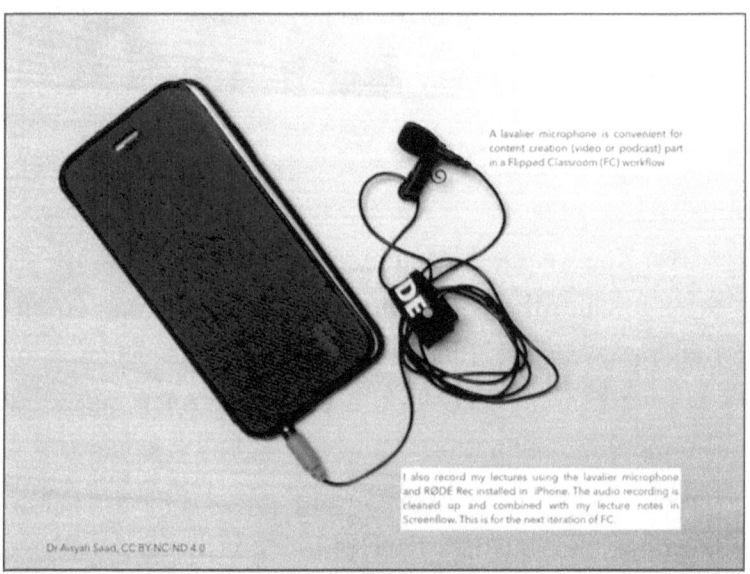

I was shy. My first video was a simple video lecture using Keynote with a voiceover. I used a lavalier microphone for the voiceover (as shown in the photo) or audio-recorded my live lectures. Then, the audio recordings were combined with my slides using Screenflow, for editing work rather than screencasting. That was the beginning of my DIY video production.

I also dislike hearing my voice, but did it anyway for my students and because I wanted to try the flipped classroom approach. I told my students to concentrate on the points in the video, but not my voice since it sounded awful.

The following week, a feedback came from my student, 'Doctor, your voice is okay. You have a nice voice.'

That simple comment extinguished my fear and insecurities with my voice. It dissolved the first psychological barrier we had been telling ourselves or what we tend to believe from others.

That simple comment extinguished my fear and insecurities with my voice.

Showing My Face

Next is whether to show my face. I deliberated on this matter for some time because one needs to look 'presentable' on camera. That was the popular thinking... And that was on the back burner until one day I was asked to represent the CDAE Director at a meeting located at the National Institute of Public Administration, better known as INTAN in Kuala Lumpur.

With one hour to pack before rushing to the airport, I knew I had to give the next day lecture a miss. To make up to my students, I decided to record a video lecture that

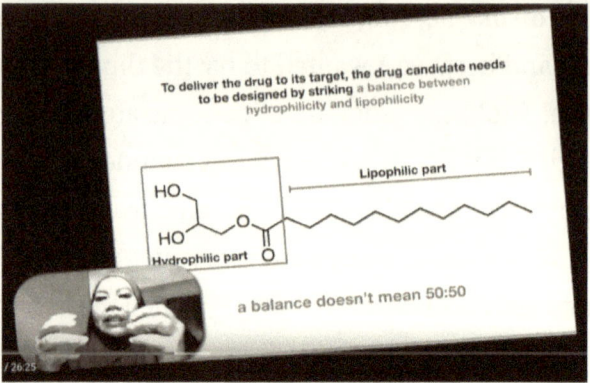

night (or rather early morning) with my webcam and in-built laptop microphone. In the manner of 'Just do it'.

That night I discovered that staring into the laptop webcam at 3 o'clock in the morning, while trying to appear interesting and presentable to the viewers, my students, is not an easy feat. Practicality presided over presentability.

Accepting my voice as it is and revealing my face are my two top psychological barriers...

Even though, I prefer 'hiding' behind the screen, I decided to 'reveal' my face since I felt it would convey a more personal feeling and connection to my students than simply a voice.

Accepting my voice as it is and revealing my face are my two top psychological barriers that I overcame in my journey of producing DIY videos.

I discovered mastering the tools are much easier now than before...

As mentioned earlier, I also wanted to find out if there is a way to do rapid DIY video production. Thanks to technology, I discovered mastering the tools are much easier now than before; though finding out what equipment suits oneself took another 6-7 months.

What are my tools behind the screen?
Why took 6-7 months? There are numerous apps and equipment for video recording, but which ones are good for you, your work and budget? Besides, to produce good quality educational videos takes some understanding of the tools and oneself, upgrading one's skills using these tools. As CDAE Trainer, I took into account finding the right ones, not just for me but also other educators. Around this time, I was creating videos for courses on Microcredential Programme@USM.

Similar to a science experiment, replicability and reproducibility are quite important in a video production process. To this end, I scoured the internet and Youtube, purchased courses on Udemy, Skillshare for practical ideas, best practices and testing out tools. I wanted to develop my own set of tools that I would feel good about and confident that over time they will deliver consistently great quality videos for educational purposes. What I aimed for was something mobile yet gives professional feels and looks.

Mobile green screen unpacked

Unpacking the bag (from clockwise): Let's start with a green fabric (A) below. You can buy the fabric from Lazada or any fabric shops e.g. Kamdar. This one I bought from Kamdar–a fabric for baju kurung. I chose a less 'shiny' and heavy fabric; this costs RM60 for 5 meters. (B) is my faithful Macbook with Screenflow installed. I also use Screencastify, Loom and Screencast-O-matic for my video production work.

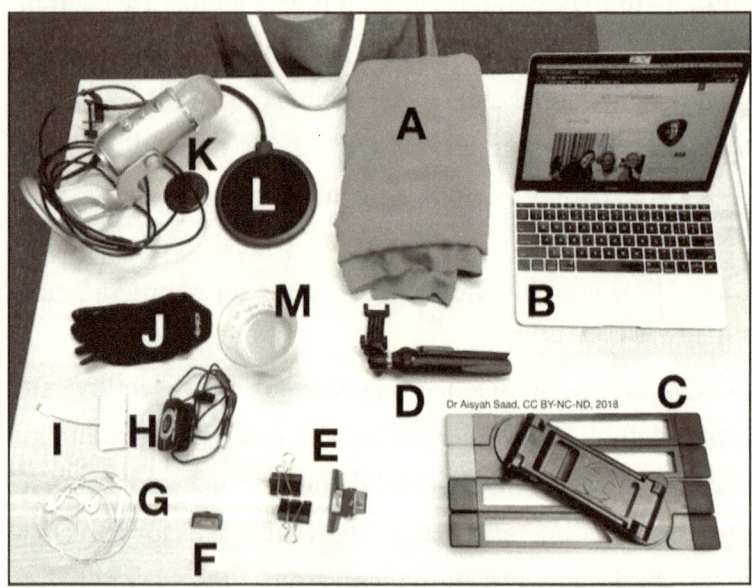

I find it is nice to place your laptop on an elevated position during screencasting. Additionally, the webcam can be at the eye-level and gives the impression to your students that you're looking at them as you speak. Scaffold (C) comes in handy for this purpose.

> *Throughout this journey, my students are my biggest supporters and critics of my videos.*

A mini tripod for a mobile phone (D) is useful if you wish to use your mobile phone for video production. Many smartphones are capable of capturing high definition (HD) resolution videos. (E) are clips to hang the green screen, (F) is a pen drive, necessary to store bulky video files. (G) is an iPhone mic/earphone that I find give great audio recording for screencasting.

(H) is a Logitech webcam, good for video production if you're on the go. I keep (H) in (J), a sock so that the webcam lens wouldn't scratch. (K) is a Blue Yeti Microphone with its pop-filter (L). I tend to use a thick sock nowadays as its pop-filter, instead of (L). And last but not least, a glass of good coffee (M) is a must to accompany any video production ;-)

My students, my inspiration
In sum, this is my mobile green screen studio—as you can see creating good quality educational videos hardly require fancy equipment. Perhaps a dash of creativity with plenty

of grit and commitment. Practice makes perfect as the saying goes.

Throughout this journey, my students are my biggest supporters and critics of my videos. I welcome suggestions and criticisms–these in turn help improve my videos. Furthermore, my students seem quite good in creating interesting videos, perhaps because they are of youtube and social media generations–the digital natives. And I learn a lot from them.

As an introverted educator, I feel the psychological barriers were the biggest hurdles to overcome than the tools mentioned above. Let me know *via* email if you have any questions or suggestions. I hope you would find this section informative and useful at the start your own journey into DIY video production.

"The journey of a thousand miles begins with one step."
–Lao Tzu

8. Epilogue

Before Elevate

"Why don't you fight?" asked a Professor when told about leaving the university.
Prof... There is no use fighting. I want to put my energy into something constructive, something good.
"What are your plans?" many colleagues enquired.
I don't know. I have no plans. Perhaps to travel first.
They were puzzled, surprised and shocked by my nonchalant answers.

• • •

I was not able to explain further, but back then, I knew I had to move on. I had this strong feeling that the path would open for me.

I had no inkling that I would write a book on presentations. As we speak, I trust my feelings and the process. One thing led to another. Things unfolded beautifully. My heart started to sing, feeling content and at peace as I write out these stories from my experiences. I used to serve as an educator and university trainer in presentations and online courses.

Somehow these stories need to be told, lessons shared– giving birth to the book 'Elevate'. It is my intention and hope that this book will guide and inspire you to the next level in academic presentations.

Trust to Elevate

Trust that you are enough. Trust that you are *already* here for a purpose. In a fast-paced world of KPIs, we sometimes forgot to trust. We forgot to allow the flow of the universe to take ourselves in the natural course of life. *To fly.*

Like an eagle that flies high in the sky. It will never fly with the low flyers, a sparrow. An eagle knows its rightful place, so does a sparrow.

Recently, I had a chat with my sister about how planes fly. She taught me the importance of aerodynamic design of a plane or a fighter jet. It's inspired by the aerodynamic shape of a bird. The aerodynamic design of an aircraft spreads the flow of air efficiently, thus allows the force of lift to push the plane up, against the gravity. With enough thrust (or trust, pun intended) to overcome drag, the plane can move forward. Aerodynamic designs assist the lift on takeoffs, and during flight—for both birds and aircraft.

Likewise, crafting a well-designed presentation will reduce the drag, get your points across to lift you and your cause higher than before. A presentation that not only informs, educates and inspires your audience, but also illuminates them in the path to success.

Trust gives you the wings to elevate above the rest.

Resources on presentation (that I love)

1. 100 Things Every Designer Needs to Know About People, Susan Weinschenk, Pearson Education, 2011. *Highly recommended.*

2. Better Presentations, Jonathan Schwabish Columbia University Press, 2016.

3. Confessions of a Public Speaker, Scott Berkun O'Reilly Media, Inc., 2009. *Recommended.*

4. Peak Performance Presentations: How to Present with Passion and Purpose: Tools and Techniques from the Stage, Richard Olivier & Nicholas Janni, Articulate Press, 2007. *Recommended.*

5. Presentation Patterns: Techniques for Crafting Better Presentations, Neal Ford, Matthew McCullough & Nathaniel Schutta, Addison-Wesley, 2012.

6. Presentation Zen: Simple Ideas on Presentation Design and Delivery, Garr Reynolds, New Riders, 2nd Ed., 2011. *Highly recommended.*

7. Presentation Zen Design: Simple Design Principles and Techniques to Enhance Your Presentations, Garr Reynolds, New Riders, 2010. *Highly recommended.*

8. Presenting to Win, The Art of Telling Your Story Jerry Weissman, Prentice Hall, 2006. *Recommended.*

9. Resonate: Present Visual Stories that Transform Audiences, Nancy Duarte, John Wiley & Sons, 2013.

10. Illuminate: Ignite Change Through Speeches, Stories, Ceremonies, and Symbols, Nancy Duarte, Portfolio, 2016.

11. Slide:ology: The Art and Science of Creating Great Presentations, Nancy Duarte, O'Reilly Media, 2008. *Highly recommended.*

12. Say it Like Obama and Win!: The Power of Speaking with Purpose and Vision, Revised and Expanded Third Edition, Shel Leanne McGraw Hill Professional, 2012.

13. Show and Tell: How Everybody Can Make Extraordinary Presentations, Dan Roam, Penguin, 2014. *Highly recommended.*

14. Talk Like TED: The 9 Public Speaking Secrets of the World's Top Minds, Carmine Gallo, Pan Macmillan, 2014. *Recommended.*

15. Teaching *for* Learning : 101 intentionally designed education activities to put students on the path to success, Claire Howell Major Routledge, Taylor & Francis, 2016. *See Chapter 1, The lecture method. Recommended.*

16. TED Talks: The official TED guide to public speaking: Tips and tricks for giving unforgettable speeches and presentations, Chris Anderson, Hachette, 2016.

17. The Forty Rules of Love: a Novel of Rumi, Elif Shafak, Penguin Books, 2011. *Recommended.*

18. The Naked Presenter: Delivering Powerful Presentations with Or Without Slides, Garr Reynolds, New Riders, 2011.

19. The Non-designer's Presentation Book: Principles for Effective Presentation Design, Robin Williams, Peachpit Press, 2010. *Recommended.*

20. The Storyteller's Secret: How TED Speakers and Inspirational Leaders Turn Their Passion Into Performance, Carmine Gallo Pan Macmillan, 2018. *Recommended.*

21. The Zen Of Creativity: Cultivating Your Artistic Life John Daido Loori, Ballantine Books, 2005.

• • •

Photos

Left photo: Professor Muhammad Yunus' talk 'A World of Three Zeros' at Dewan Budaya, Universiti Sains Malaysia. Right photo: Thanks Powerpoint! The picture with Prof. Yunus was a pure coincidence. When he arrived, the organiser ushered him to a seat in front of me. While the organiser was sorting out their Powerpoint presentation, I asked him for a quick picture. He happily obliged my request and placed his hand over mine in a fatherly manner. That reminds me of my late dad. It's been over a decade—miss him terribly... *Al-Fatihah*.

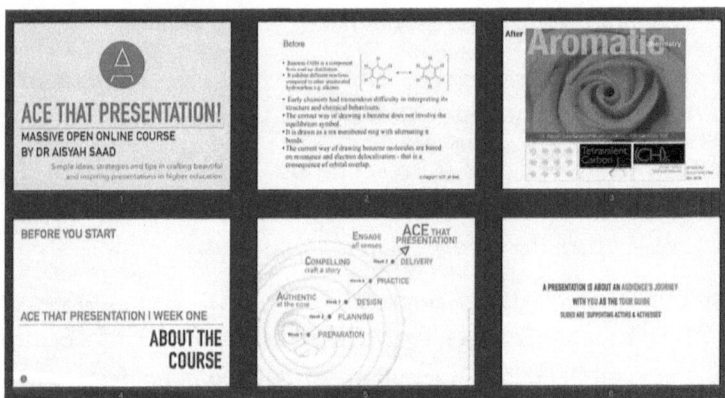

Above is the first 6 slides for a MOOC 'ACE That Presentation'. It was designed entirely in Apple Keynote. Shown here are the title slide followed by 'Before' and 'After' examples of 'Aromatic Chemistry' teaching slides. The half-cut onion serves as a framework for the MOOC, where one starts from inside out. That is, starting from the core (Week 1: Preparation, Being Authentic) and work your way to delivery (Week 5, Engaging delivery through all senses). Keep slides simple and clear of any clutter allow your message to shine through.

Penicillin balloons in-class activity

Clockwise from top left: A student counting how many 'hotdogs' to twist before tying up to form a ring. I like going around the lecture hall and address a smaller group of students. Explaining to the entire class how penicillin's shape relates to its action using a huge penicillin balloon model.

Teaching with tech. Clockwise from top left: Green screen setup in my old office with a mobile studio bag carrying all things needed to produce a good quality video (the second photo). The third photo shows a simple setup for an online discussion with students using Facebook Live.

An email from a Presentation Zen reader provides a strong motivation to continue the effort in elevating academic presentations.

" ...found your presentation "Aromatic Chemistry" on Slideshare. This is such a good presentation. It is exactly what I am trying to tell the students. Get rid of the bullet points and use pictures!...

Dr Terese Bergfors
Co-editor of Acta Cryst F
Uppsala University, Sweden
http://xray.bmc.uu.se/terese/

Acknowledgements

I feel privileged and fortunate to have worked with passionate and brilliant colleagues from various backgrounds—not only in pharmacy, health and life sciences, but also from education, economics, computer sciences, social sciences, management, engineering and in e-learning scenes, *viz.* Malaysia e-Learning Council (MEIPTA), throughout my academic career.

Many of the acquaintances and collaborators have blossomed into friendship. Not forgetting my friends, near and far; you know who you are. Thank you for your support, intellectual discourses and counsels. To my pharmacy students, I learned so much from you. Stay awesome! Lastly, my deepest gratitude to my family for your love, encouragement and support throughout this journey.

www.ingramcontent.com/pod-product-compliance
Lightning Source LLC
Chambersburg PA
CBHW030636220526
45463CB00004B/1540